JOHN ZORN
THE BOOK OF HEADS

Andrea Aguzzi

Copyright © 2020 by Andrea Aguzzi

Cover Copyright © 2020 by Nicola Aguzzi

All rights reserved. This book or any portion thereof may not be reproduced or used in any manner whatsoever without the express written permission of the publisher except for the use of brief quotations in a book review or scholarly journal.

First Printing: 2020

Editing: Serena Bonaventura

978-1-71693-224-3
Imprint: Lulu.com

Via Passo Pordoi 13
30173 Venezia Italy

https://neuguitars.com/

To Serena and Nicola

Contents

Foreword by Alessandra Novaga..7

The beginning...11

JOHN ZORN..17
John Zorn: Gomi no Sensei...19
Composition..33
Improvisation..58

THE BOOK OF HEADS..75
John Zorn and Agatha Christie..77
The 70s...84
New York, New York..95
Doctor Eugene Chadbourne..105
Musical theater: Theatre of Musical Optics................................110
Traditional score against graphic notation.................................113
The score..116
The Book of Heads and the open work......................................123

Urban and musical congestion..126

The end..129

Acknowledgments..131

Discography..133

Bibliography...135

Foreword by Alessandra Novaga

Andrea asked me to write something that introduces his book on John Zorn and his Book Of Heads, and I thought that if he asked me it wasn't for my skills as an essayist, but because, in the 2012, I did some concerts where I performed the opera in its full version. So, since the book is really a very accurate and passionate essay, I will not try to analyze the Book Of Heads, but I will try to talk about it from my point of view, from the point of view of someone who has got her hands on it, and in this case also the feet, if I can say so...
After listening to the magnificent edition played by Marc Ribot, I ordered the scores, and these small cards arrived, on each one there was a study that looked like a miniature, written in ink, and a legend to decipher the symbols. I started to work on it a bit, but the undertaking seemed rather difficult, especially because until then I had only attended the world of written scores. The only experience I had besides the classical guitar, was playing Trash TV Trance by Fausto Romitelli, thanks to which I bought my first electric guitar and all the equipment to perform it.
Shortly afterwards I found myself in New York, in a coffee bar, with my friend James Moore, who had just played all of them at the Anthology Film Archives, and who encouraged me to face them, "You'll see, it's really a journey", he told me, and so, as soon as I got back to Milan, I bought some different guitars, and I got serious about it.
And it was truly a journey, an incredible opportunity to speculate around the idea of guitar. Zorn does not give indications on which type to use for this or that study, therefore understanding the flow of different sounds, given by the different guitars, is a difficult but stimulating undertaking, especially if you face the work in its entirety. I used five different ones, and it was not easy to find the space in the house to be able to recreate the necessary set, not to mention the amount of balloons that I had to inflate every day, during the preparation period! Going back to the idea of a travel, I think it is extremely interesting to do it, first of all trying to

understand what the scores say, what Zorn wants to tell us.

To quote Marc Ribot, "Zorn is a true composer, he knows more about extending tecnique on guitar than I do. Sometimes he writes things that are impossible to do, but that's okay because he does it intentionally." In my opinion this thought unlocks the whole interpretative operation; it must be understood that the relationship you establish with those cards and their hieroglyphics must be absolutely personal. It makes no sense to ask the composer for explanations. You have to find your way, and the further you go the more the fog unravels. Then the proportion between the improvised freedom, that you have to take, and the written sign that traces you a way, becomes reality.

While I was immersed in the preparation of The Book Of Heads, my idea was increasingly outlined compared to the fact that when it was decided to move from tablature to modern notation, we have acquired greater precision in understanding the idea of the composer and a certain executive practicality, but we have also lost that spontaneity, that instinct and that thought/hands adherence, which we can only find today in jazz musicians.

For me, who until then I had only moved in the field of exact notation, The Book Of Heads was an opportunity to draw on a series of intuitions, and more compositional than interpretative skills, and this helped me a lot to broaden my horizons. The playful aspect is also very important, but I think it's also important not to ridicule them too much; you use dolls that speak, bursts or rubs balloons, mumble even, in some studies, but, especially if you deal with the work in its entirety, you understand that they are all pieces that actually help us to understand our contemporaneity in its many facets.

They help us to compare the various musical traditions, our sense of humor and the tragic, how far our interpretative skills go, and how far our autonomy of thought and, this means a lot, our physical reflexes. Shortly, it's not a small thing, if we think that all this is contained in a single work. I think it's very nice to 'see them' play, because the gestures and all the instrumental changes that take place are an integral part of the work. It's a real show! If I think that when I played them I went around the world with five guitars, an amplifier, two suitcases and a bag full of various tools!!!

Alessandra Novaga

The beginning

"Composed from 1976-1978 and now studied by guitarists the world over, The Book of Heads is one of Zorn's most popular and oft-performed composition."[1]

"Marc Ribot guitar solo
3 dicembre 1999, ore 21.00
Venezia, Aula Magna IUAV, Tolentini, Santa Croce 191
"Uno dei più famosi ed acclamati chitarristi della scena "alternativa" mondiale, collaboratore fisso di John Zorn e Tom Waits, in un solo concerto in cui tutta la maestria e lo swing di un grande musicista possono scatenarsi, tra standards e improvvisazione, tra canzoni e improvvise accelerazioni."[2]

This was the presentation of Marc Ribot's concert on the website of the Venetian association Vortice[3]. I still have a distinct memory of that concert. The Aula Magna was crowded with fans and Ribot presented himself with a true avant-garde guitarist's set: several guitars that he changed quickly with each song and that he could play at the same time, a small fan prepared with elastic bands instead of the usual blades with which he hit directly the strings, a violin bow and on the ground inflated balloons to burst with his feet rhythmically during the songs or to rub on the fretboard and on the guitar strings.
I remember a fun evening. Ribot was in great shape and alternated jazz,

---

[1] Notes from the obi of the cd "John Zorn James Moore Plays The Book of Heads", Tzadik, 2015.
[2] "One of the most famous and acclaimed guitarists of the "alternative" world scene, a strong collaborator of John Zorn and Tom Waits, in a single concert where all the mastery and swing of a great musician can be unleashed, between standards and improvisation, between songs and sudden accelerations."
[3] The link is still available: http://vortice.provincia.venezia.it/Ribot.html

rock and blues with very short interludes where he "tortured" the guitar with the bow, the balloons or scrambling in any possible way. Despite the presence of many young people, the public reacted to this wave of amusing anarchy with the compassionate and heavy attitude that you can, sometimes, see in the public of avant-garde concerts. Not a laugh, not a smile in front of the obvious irony shown by Ribot himself. What a pity!

A few years later, driven by my usual guitar curiosity, I bought the album "The Book of Heads" by John Zorn and finally found out what those short musical sketches with which Ribot interspersed his concert were: they were part of the 35 studios composed by Zorn, played and recorded in 1995 by Ribot himself and dedicated to and inspired by Eugene Chadbourne.

It wasn't the first time I met Zorn's music, I had listened to "Spillane" in 1989 at a friend's house and I was impressed. A few years later I came across Naked City, listening to their first self-titled album and to "Torture Garden" and it was love at first listening, a truly stimulating experience. Slowly, Zorn's music has become one of my favorite obsessions, to understand it better I bought and listened to tons of other music, read books, searched for interviews, talked to many musicians. Eventually all these experiences condensed in this book. I hope it will be useful to all those who wish to play this music and to those who love John Zorn and the guitar.

Why should I write an essay, a sort of a "manifesto" about some graphic scores, about some guitar's studies in an era that disdains "manifestos"? The Book of Heads are a curious thing: a mountain of concreteness without a manifesto. We are talking about an almost brazen musical architecture: composition and improvisation together, a musical architecture loved in a measure directly proportional to its absolute lack of aversion for itself and respected precisely for the historical excesses through which The Book of Heads were developed. They shows a series of strategies, theorems, and achievements that not only confer a logic and a structure to Zorn's past musical development but an uninterrupted validity and vitality capable of transcending his New York origins to claim a role among the most interesting contemporary musical theories. I started to get interested in contemporary guitar music in 2007. Now I can say that it was a natural outlet, an obvious and compelling need. I needed new ideas to survive. I needed new spaces to explore and grow. I've always been a guitar fanatic. At that time it seemed to me that the musical genres I used to frequent, my musical gardens, my playing fields, rock, jazz, blues, folk and classical had exhausted their potential and that a cultural retreat on static positions, on known and well-practiced aesthetics, had begun. Those perimeters were starting to get tight. The Book of Heads seem to me the perfect guide to enter this new, exciting musical world, teeming with life and new forms. The first thing I did was to go in search of a music scene.

Why should it be so strange? All those who come from rock, jazz, blues, popular music dream of meeting a new music scene. The "music scene" is the Holy Grail. The pure desire of every enthusiast. The quantum leap for those who write about music. But I quickly discovered that in contemporary music, or in avant-garde music, or in experimental music things are not so simple. In these areas, in these territories there are no real musical scenes. Not in the sense in which we are used to considering them in the world of popular music. A little at time, I learned that contemporary music, avant-garde music, experimental music do not sound exactly as synonyms, but as aesthetic and marketing categories quite confused with each other and that their boundaries are as wide as they are unexplored. In addition, in recent years the concept of the music scene as previously defined has disappeared. Thanks to globalization and the possibilities of interaction offered by internet and social networks, only a few realities have managed to maintain a leading role as cultural attractors for creative phenomena and subcultures: New York, Tokyo, perhaps even London...the suburbs have almost disappeared. At the same time, continuing to deepen the fields of improvisation and composition, I realized how The Book of Heads were exactly at the center of a complex network of cultural relationships linked to these subcultures. When The Book of Heads were created music scenes were still a well-established phenomenon, especially in such a dynamic and troubled reality as New York was. And within these subcultures, The Book of Heads could be considered not only the fruit of Zorn's creativity but also the result of a more complex web of relationships, connected implicitly or explicitly to Zorn himself. To better understand them, I have repeatedly resorted to the concept of "scenius", a neologism born from the fusion of the terms scene and genius, coined by Brian Eno, to indicate an artistic phenomenon linked to a collective scene rather than to a single person[4].

I think that a composition, a piece must work on many different levels. It must be something that can be brought closer to the more immediate, simpler level and then beyond this evident level there should be more subtle, complex levels. Experimental music has now been able to create its own language, partly derived from the tradition, partly new. A phenomenon that has very deep origins, not only musical but also political and social. Nowadays there is a musical pluralism and my pleasure and duty is to navigate between these languages looking for the threads that holds them together. Zorn and The Book of Heads are great examples. Personally I do not conceive history in a deterministic way, as a series of facts that occur because there has been a cause that has produced certain effects. In music there is not that linearity of development that allows science (a very light vision of science) to make predictions on the basis of acquired experiences and data. Like any form of creativity, The Book of Heads are more than just an individual fact. Creation needs dialogue, interlocutors and music also needs interpreters in the most concrete sense of the term. But the interpreters do not invent themselves, as the public is not invented: they are part of a cultural and evolutionary process that implies a dialogue, which is not always peaceful. The composer, the interpreter and the listener do not belong to different socio-cultural categories. All three produce culture. The Book of Heads are the demonstration of how musical languages are not invented:

---

[4] See Brian Eno talking about "scenius" at 'Basic Income: How do we get there?' Basic Income UK meet-up at St Clements Church Kings Square, London, 3 December 2015. Link: https://youtu.be/qkD7JBspgas

they are formed and transformed, under all sorts of influences, even extraneous to music. Art is not deaf to history. The civil world, whatever the catastrovists and revisionists think and despites all its crises, transforms and changes like a living body: it elaborates symbols, living languages and objects to show its existence. The artist is the first to be immersed in it and creates not only for himself, but also for his civilized world, for its lights and shadows. Today's music is not made only with notes. A musical form like The Book of Heads is first of all a testimony, an evidence and not only a mood to be perceived, nor a pattern to be analyzed with philological scruple. Categorical statements such as right or wrong, beautiful or ugly are no longer suitable for understanding how and why a composer works today on audible forms and musical action. The Book of Heads cannot be considered a closed, precise and comfortable system, where everything happens in a predetermined way, but rather a branched system of sounds and actions, definable and meaningful only in reality and in the decisions and relationships that they imply at the time of their execution . Eventually, they became a small, pleasant obsession.

JOHN ZORN

John Zorn: Gomi no Sensei

"Rubin, in some way that no one quite understands, is a master, a teacher, what the Japanese call a sensei. What he's the master of, really, is garbage, kipple, refuse, the sea of cast-off goods our century floats on. Gomi no sensei. Master of junk."[5]

John Zorn (New York, September 2, 1953) is one of the most prolific and influential musicians of his generation, perhaps the last of the great Dadaist and postmodern experimenters. Composer[6], saxophonist, improviser, producer, creator and holder of the independent record label Tzadik, as well as talented talent scout, John Zorn is one of the key figures of New York's musical alternative scene. Probably his best-known areas are contemporary and avant-garde music: among his most well-known projects are the jazz-kletzmer experimental group Masada and the super-group Naked City. Featuring a total curiosity for everything that is "new", a Renaissance eclecticism and an incontrovertible record prolificity, he has worked with many musicians, especially in improvised

---

[5] Burning Chrome, William Gibson , Orion Publishing Group, London, 2016 in "Winter Market" pag. 127.

[6] In this book the noun "composer" is used by referring to the definition used by Adam Harper in his book "Infinite Music Imaging the next Millenium of Human Music Making", pag. 7: "A 'composer'...is routinely held to be a specially trained person (usually a man) who writes music using Western classical notation, which is then given to an ensemble of specially trained musicians playing Western classical instruments.But technically the world 'composer' suggests anyone at all who might create music.In this sense, the term overlaps with the word 'performer'... with the word 'composer' I'll be referring to any source of music at all, multiple or otherwise, including performers (they be singers or instrumentalists), producers, singer-songwriters, 'artists', sound artist, Djs and other selectors, artificial sources adn even, in a significant sense, people who play music to themselves alone, with instrument or the press of a button."

music, blending together contemporary music, jazz and rock (even death metal and grindcore), making stylistic nomadism one of his fundamental traits. At the same time as a musician he has been able to define a new style for his saxophone, a style similar to the punk-rock guitar, defined by critics as jazz-punk and also as jazz-slatter.

John Zorn began studying piano and flute when he was almost ten years old, then he played guitar and when he was fourteen he began composing and discovering a true passion for contemporary classic music. In the following years he studied at the St. Louis College, played the saxophone and fell in love with free jazz, especially Antony Braxton. After leaving the college, he moved to New York, where he began to come into contact with the vivid and impetuous avant-garde Downtown scene. Here he began his career: he played in all kinds of bands, from jazz to rock, from avant-garde to free improvisation.

If there is something that can easily irritate him, it's surely the usual habit of both music criticism and music business to attribute a label to any artist, which for Zorn is the greatest dislike. This is evident in his preface to the first book of the Arcana series, which he wrote himself:

"Rock. Jazz. Punk. Dada. Beat. These words and their longer cousins, the ismfamily (surrealism, postmodernism, abstract expressionism, minimalism), are used to commodify and commercialize an artist's complex personal vision. This terminology is not about understanding. It never has been. It's about money."[7]

Assigning a label it's not only an easy mean of presenting a record, a music, a musician on the market, but it's also for consumerism. Once a certain label has been affixed to a work, to a music, the listener has no need to "listen to" it, since he is already prepared for an elaborate system of judgments and values.[8] In practice, criticism eventually ends up

---

[7] "Arcana Musicians on Music" edited by John Zorn, Granary Books/Hips Road, 2000, pag. V.
[8] "Composers don't think in terms of boxes and genres. They just do what they

mentioning itself. On the contrary, Zorn strives to surprise his listeners, his fans continually tearing off their soft and comfortable limbo.

"Once a group of artists, writers, or musicians has been packaged together under such a banner, it is not only easier for work to be marketed - it also becomes easier for the audience to 'buy it' and for the critic to respond with pre-packaged opinions. The audience is deprived of its right to the pleasure of creating its own interpretation, and the critic no longer has to think about what is really happening or go any deeper than the monochromatic surface of the label itself, thus avoiding any encounter with the real aesthetic criteria that make any individual artist's work possible."[9]

With his music, the listener has to create his own interpretations based on his own aesthetic criterias, not according to the values that are proposed with the music business's label . The music industry's classification system is not the only object of Zorn's strals, he also likes to shout against prejudices and elitisms in music criticism: the notion of a distinction between "high" and "low art" is simply "a bunch of fucking bullshit". It's taking into account these ideas and basics that we will move along this book. My goal is to create a map, to help define better his complex stylistic territory so that the readers can then independently create their own path to approach, understand and manage the complex Zorn's universe.
I just ask you to keep in mind that Zorn is accustomed to expressing his opinions with definite "rude and unpolite" terms:

"That's the kind of thing created to make it look like you listen to

---

do, and they love good music, whatever hits them. It doesn't matter where it comes from, who's doing it, or what it's trying to say." Ann McCutchan "The Muse That Sings: Composers Speak About the Creative Process ", Oxford University Press, 2003 pag. 163.

[9] "Arcana musicians on music", cit., pag. V.

classical music while you're sipping champagne and with rock music you're boogeying [sic] with a bottle of beer and jazz you're in some dirty club with a shot of whiskey or some shit like that…There's good music and great music and phoney music in every genre and all the genres are the fucking same! Classical music is not better than blues because this guy went to school and got a degree and studied very cleanly while the other guy was out on the street living it."[10]

Even if all this smells like relativism, Zorn has chosen to play, compose, and produce only music that transports him spiritually. Nothing is excluded, as long as it is sincere and is done with consistency and commitment. And although some styles like grindcore, hard be bop, cartoon music are closer to Zorn's heart and reflect themselves on his music (especially in Naked City and Painkiller), he doesn't seem to attribute a greater or a lesser importance to a style than to another, his influences and interests are, as his music, incredibly varied. He writes in the notes accompanying the record "Spillane":

"I grew up in New York City as a media freak, watching movies and TV and buying hundreds of records. There's a lot of jazz in me, but there's also a lot of rock, a lot of classical, a lot of ethnic music, a lot of blues, a lot of movie soundtracks. I'm a mixture of all those things…We should take advantage of all the great music and musicians in this world without fear of musical barriers, which sometimes are even stronger than racial or religious ones.[11]"

Why is Zorn a "Gomi no Sensei"? I chose this definition to characterize this book thanks to a very poetic tale written by the cyberpunk science fiction writer William Gibson.
In "Winter Market", a small tale with a great atmosphere, there is Rubin,

---

[10] Interview with Edward Strickland. Link: https://groups.google.com/forum/#!topic/rec.music.bluenote/V4TBWloL7No
[11] From the booklet of the cd Spillane, pag.10.

a Japanese artist, a junk master: "What he's the master of, really, is garbage, kipple, refuse, the sea of cast-off goods our century floats on."[12] The same nickname was also tagged by Delany to Gibson himself, who defined it precisely as a gomi no sensei: a 'bricoleur' writer, one who puts a lot of different stuff, a lot of junk inside his writings.

Gomi is a Japanese word that means garbage or dust, but it's also used to describe anything we discard or to which we no longer value. Gibson uses the word gomi to describe the cultural distopia of our society in a closer future, not so difficult to imagine.

It's the "Blade Runner"'s world, in which monumental garbage mountains eclipse the landscape to become the ground on which human creatures build their lives. Gibson asks to ourselves where gomi ends and where the world begins. Rubin, the artist, seems to have solved and overcome this dichotomy. In his creative laboratory he mixes these scraps of different materials, he doesn't think about them as garbage, but for him they are his mediums, the air he breathes, the cultural tides in which he has always been immersed. The materials he uses are common ground, once they were raw materials, transformed into technology, discarded as garbage, rediscovered by the artist's eye, gomi become the foundation for his works, for his art, such as the small objects placed inside the Joseph Cornell's boxes[13]. The medium becomes the message.

Son (as Zappa was) of an age where you can have easily access, thanks to internet, records, youtube, mp3 and streaming channels, to any kind of music, Zorn is an avid records' collector and he is the founder one of the most interesting labels dedicated to avant-garde music, the Tzadik.

Being a musical gomi no Sensei and the heir of a contemporary sort of Zappa's"Lumpy Gravy", Zorn contains some of the peculiar features that marked our age and our way of making (and listening to) music:

---

[12] William Gibson, cit.
[13] On Cornell's influence on Zorn's music, read John Brackett's "John Zorn Tradition and Transgression", Indiana University Press, 2008, p. 100-104.

- John Zorn is the contemporary composer who has better managed and interpolated some of the features of the world we live in: syncretic accumulation, media manipulation, kinematic music, design and advertising, annulment of temporal dimension, daily neurosis, violence;
- he is a "media freak", a cinema, cartoons and tv shows' fanatic;
- he has developed a strong interest in Japanese music and culture;
- he has his own view about yiddish and kletzmer music and of his own Jewish identity;
- he considers the use of noise as a constructive element of his music;
- he sees his role as a composer as a "problem solver" as a non-alien figure but integrated into the society in which he lives;
- his compositions (and improvisations) are the result of a creative process built up with a team of musicians, specially chosen to record that specific piece music and to stimulate it so that they can add to its realization their intuitions, skills and specificities;
- the absolute refusal to use "tape editing" techniques in the studio, firm determination in doing it all "the hard way" in the classical way, by trying and retrying every step until it's perfect, costing to become a dictator ;
- absolute and total respect for Carl Stalling and Igor Strawinsky and their block composition method, developed by the "file cards"'s method.

Zorn's musical gomi breaks the rules, but at the same time assumes its own responsibilities by striving to give new life to existing, dated materials, technologies and musics. The result is avant-garde music, but it doesn't distance the listener accustomed to consumer music.
Zorn's gomi is not nostalgic, he doesn't want to bring back the clock or embrace New Age philosophies. It's the exact opposite. He was born and feeds himself thanks to New York's gotham city, thanks to its cultural crossover, to its frantic daily activity, its infinite cultural, technological, racial and musical stimulations.
It's pure DIY. He expresses an economic-artistic self-sufficiency mentality based on the consciousness that we live in very hard, dark ages. He is conducives to technology and its creative use, thinking and reusing

music and 'second hand' solutions in a new way.
Cars, motorcycles, medias, energy production, humanity's evolution, personal technology, music, communication, sense of community, new aesthetics, magics, Internet. All things without which we can't now live and that are embraced by gomi, a desire for change, for improvement, for rebirth. Zorn's gomi is the result of a precise and consistent aesthetic choice: his best defense against unreasonable mediocrity and his music expresses a constant tension through the unconscious and subversive use of precise structures approachable to academic music combined with elements coming from popular and underground music. Rightly writes John Lowell Brackett in his excellent Zorn's book:

" It's not that Zorn's music "lacks" deep structures but that the notion of deep structure itself is revealed as specious and, as a concept, is devoid of any sort of justification other than tradition and prejudice. Seen from this perspective, Zorn's musical practices proudly display the leaking sewer pipes and termite-infested edifice that used to support the ivory tower."[14]

An elegant and diplomatic way to solve the analysis's difficulties inherent in Zorn's music might be to insert them into the conceptual / theoretical postmodernism's framework[15]. In fact this is what happened in the few academic essays written about Zorn, where the term 'postmodernism' is invoked in order to better explain the juxtapositions and incongruences that characterize his 'musical surfaces'. Renée T. Coulombe, for example, defines Spillane as *"landmark postmodern piece for its sonic juxtapositions of disjunct materials:"*[16].
For Jonathan Kramer, Forbidden Fruit represents a form of radical postmodernism by offering *"considerable dose of postmodern chaos,*

---

[14] John Lowell Brackett "John Zorn: tradition and transgression", Indiana University Press, 2008, pag xii.
[15] Kenneth Gloag, Postmodernism in Music, pag.100.
[16] John Lowell Brackett,cit., pag. xiii.

despite its nostalgia for other musics"[17]

Personally, I do not think this is correct, or rather I do not think the postmodernist's eye can be considered the only reading's key. First of all, I think this definition can only apply to some of Zorn's music, those built using the blocks's methos and the Naked City's music, but not for example the Masada corpus, magic-related and esoteric music, improvisations and games pieces, all the grind core things and the Painkiller's noise. Secondly, I have doubts that composing a music characterized by fragmented and fragmented elements automatically gives the right to regard it as postmodern.

I think rather than the specifics and particular characteristics of his music require separate calibrated analyzes on specific and, alas, provisional features. Zorn's music magma is constantly and unceasingly moving, we are talking about a composer / improviser / entrepreneur / producer / cultural animator / publisher...whose main feature seems to be an incredible creative worker and having a huge creative power, perfectly integrated into the neuroticism and chaotic New York's art scene[18].

In this book I propose therefore to assimilate it to the character of

---

[17] "Listening to Forbidden Fruit can be as dizzying as it is electrifying. You never know what is coming next, nor when. The stylistic juxtapositions are amazingly bold. If there were any discernible thread of continuity, the music would surely be more tame, more predictable, more ordinary. But there is not."Jonathan Kramer, Beyond Unity, pag. 22.

[18] "That's who I am. For instance, I just got off the phone with the census bureau and they asked me how many hours do I work in a week. And my answer, basically, was I work 24 hours a day. Even when I'm sleeping I'm working. I'm talking with you, I'm working. I get up first thing in the morning, the computer goes on, I'm answering e-mails. I go out to lunch, I have a discussion with someone, it's about music, it's about art. I go to a museum. Even in the cab I'm on the phone doing business. I'm always working. My life is making work. That's why I'm here. People are surprised that it's possible to get as much work done as I do. It's very simple. I choose to work. I don't go on a vacation. I'm not interested in that." John Zorn: The Working Man by Bill Milkowski, JazzTimes May 2009.

William Gibson's novel and to examine, step by step, some specific features so that each of us can create his own personal analysis path by building a cultural and cognitive map of Zorn's musical territory .
So I thought about writing this book both as a building and as a map, looking for the expression of a territorial geography. A building in which each chapter represents a different plane, an autonomous yet interconnected form in which the reader moves between one part to another as in an architectural space noting the repetition of some constructive elements: some themes that I simply sketched in a chapter can become carriers a bit further.
To do this I used two fundamental approaches. I decided to use one of Zorn's favorite compositional methods, the"file cards", combining records and cds from his extensive discography, creating paths between different music, drawing different cognitive maps that can be summed up and merging them into a sort of astral three-dimensional geography, an architecture of thoughts, reflections, emotions. I use cinema, Zorn's great passion, to find elements that provided the starting and development bases of these paths where cd covers can become the frames of a film whose mounting I hope has the power to generate and define new emotions.
In doing so, I have always confronted my personal ideas with the statements made by Zorn during his sporadic interviews. If his relationship with the press and the media can't be sure defined as idyllic, it's also true that the saxophonist, when he decides to talk, is more than willing to speak with great frankness and no turnarounds, as he likes to leave precise traces of his work in the booklets and covers of his records, where he often and willingly synthesizes the bases of his work[19].
John Zorn is all this, without forgeting his sense of irony, his the meta-linguistic plays, the free trans-testuality and unmanageable hypertextuality, both often blatantly exposed, even more radical than the

---

[19] In particular, this is the essence of the DVD documentary "A Bookshelf on Top of the Sky: 12 Stories About John Zorn", directed by Claudia Heuermann.

"cut and paste" offered by the diffusion and almost daily circulation of those DIY digital techniques that, just a few years ago, were exclusive uses for people into electronic avant-garde music both on the side of the pure academic, concrète and electroacoustic music, as well as the popular with the development of the creative possibilities offered by the recording studio (just think about Dub, Kraut rock and hip hop). If Zorn's bricolage, his personal re-elaboration of musical and cultural gomi differs from these practices, it's not so much for his form but for the substance: his transversality, intertestuality and hypertextuality has a strong "analogical" flavor, is rooted in the text of his scores, which he uses as a development tool within a narrow, almost initiatic circle of musicians friends.

Almost all of Zorn's music has a pre-existing text as a starting point, not necessarily or exclusively musical, but with a programmatic structure that proceeds coherently from concepts, themes, objects and inspirational subjects, applies true formulas and follows rigid self-imposed rules. As in the Naked City's composing workshop ("how many different music can you play with the same rock ensemble?"); the Ornette Coleman's tribute (Spy vs. Spy, 1986) is the result of a the free jazz and punk equation; Masada as a union of free jazz and klezmer; Painkiller of free jazz, dub and grindcore; the game pieces (the most famous being Cobra, 1987) as a structure of collective improvisation, etc.

Umberto Eco rightly writes in his book "The Name of the Rose": "Then comes the time when the (modern) avant-garde can no longer go any further, because it has now produced a metallic language that speaks of its impossible texts (conceptual art). The postmodern response to modernity is to recognize that the past, since it can't be destroyed, because its destruction leads to silence, must be revisited: with irony, not in an innocent way."[20]

This compositional-improvisational structure often moves towards the boundaries of a possible form characterized by a personal semiotic translation/reworking of the original starting shapes. Zorn always permits

---

[20] Umberto Eco, Il nome della Rosa, Bompiani, 1985 pag. 529 (translation is mine)

the rebuilt of all these sources, providing the listener with all the starting points using prefabricated material's forms: records' titles, individual songs's titles, images and cover graphics, liner notes etc. Zorn inscribes his own references, and especially the devotees of his own music (which are also the inspirers), considered in all respects an integral part of the work, within the text, in a much more elaborate version then the Beatles and Frank Zappa's conceptual covers of their records.

"I think Rubin sees things in a different way, too, all the time, but for him it's a source of strenght. He lives in other people's garbage, and everything he drags home must have been new and shiny once, must have meant something, however briefly, to someone. So he sweep it all up into his crazy-looking truck and hauls it back to his place and lets it compost there until he thinks of something new to do with it."[21]

The music of Zorn's masters comes, through his mediation and his re-readings, to new listeners. The intertestual link is always present in Zorn, even when it's not offered or isn't captured in the tangle of basic dimensions and valorisations that innervate the the main focus of his works: intertestuality, or "second degree" textuality, really looks like Zorn's composing "ground zero".

I agree with Grabriele Marino when he define Zorn's music breaking it through four dimensions (writing, genre, structure, value): the first three relate to the technical-formal aspect (the records, for example), the fourth isabout the contents/aspects thematic (what records are, what values and what affective contents are communicated)[22]:

- Writing: written music; improvised music; music in part written and

---

[21] William Gibson, cit. pag. 147.
[22] Gabriele Marino, L'estasi dell'influenza: John Zorn e la transtestualità come paradigma http://www.esteticastudiericerche.com/index.php?option=com_content&view=article&id=184:lestasi-dellinfluenza-john-zorn-e-la-transtestualita-come-paradigma

partly improvised;
- Genre: music genres; transgenic music (which runs vertically and paradigmatically more genres); fusion (horizontal union, overlapping of several genres);
- Structure: block music; linear music; music in part in blocks and in part linear;
- Value: hardcore (affective content: violence); music romance (Zorn's "easy listening"), Jewish music (identity value); musicianship (technical-stylistic value); tributes.

This latter component (the tribute) within its value dimension, the presence of a (more or less explicit) devotee always informs Zorn's text, as a discourse on which all others are engaged. That is how in Zorn's production we can trace all those musics that we know to be, biographically, Zorn's love and distress from the earliest years of his life to his artistic maturity: the movies' soundtracks (Morricone, John Barry) and the cartoons' music (Carl Stalling) of his childhood; the classic-contemporary composers (Mauricio Kagel, Charles Ives, Harry Partch, Igor Stravinskij, Arnold Schönberg) of his adolescence when he played the bass in a surf-rock band, but he had already decided that he would have become a composer; the "structured" free jazz discovered at the time of college (BAG / Black Artist Group and AACM / Association for the Advancement of Creative Musicians); the free improvisation (or non-idiomatic improvisation) experimented by Derek Bailey, which is the natural, human and linguistic context in which he found himself working and in which he formed himself as a musician when he met the New York musical scene in the half of the Seventies.

Much of the possibilities of reconstructing the context in which the single Zorn's text intends to fit in, and therefore the possibility of its understanding comes from our ability to recognize the intertextual games that are subscribed to. Zorn always shows his sources, but it remains the fact that many of the textual strategies he has put in place require not only specific but decoded specific musicological competencies. Zorn claims to be creating a new model of composer and musician for this age, a "new musicianship", experimenting in particular with techniques of manipulation of pre-existing musical texts conceived when he was younger and originally intended as methods for studying and analyzing the compositions of his favorite composers. Zorn plays a double movement: he pays homage to the masters and seeks new ways to revitalize their language, the avant-garde language.

The one played by Zorn is one of the possible syntheses of the music that preceded him, and can be placed in a theory that includes very different figures such as John Cage, Luciano Berio, Miles Davis, Frank Zappa and Brian Eno, creative artists who used polidirectionalism and mistyling as their own path and their own personal languages, pre-text musicians, talking about which we ends up talking about the world, remaining out of the simple rhetoric of contamination, in a continuous tension between material analysis and their synthesis.

Zorn's synthesis is a paradoxical and in some respects disconcerting abstract, exposing diversity, contradictions, musical and cultural oppositions without seeking conciliation or re-absorption. His experimentalism is experimenting with the musical forms of the past: vivisected (Naked City), rewritten (tributes, music romance discs), merged together (Masada, Painkiller). His avant-garde idea, a still possible avanguard, is vital to explore extreme musical forms (from silence to noise, from ambient to hardcore, through serialism), and I think it should look like an "ecstasy of contrasts".

Zorn's work is a compilation, a great, partial and flawed catalog of 20th-century music, and constitutes a continuous challenge to the listener, to his decoding skills, to his memory: it's a meta-linguistic reflection about nature, the boundaries and possibilities of the musical material itself and the different musical traditions. An intimately self-explanatory music, a metamusics, a music that first speaks of itself, of its own being and its being interpreted: able to offer, beyond the satisfaction of listening, an endless series of stimuli.

And I think that all this can be heard in the extreme synthesis offered by his Book of Heads guitars solos, where John Zorn has reached the highest possible level of musical and stylistic congestion, like Ruben with his gomi.

"As for the listener, ultimately the most subjective response is the best response. Eventually, total subjectivity becomes total objectivity."[23]

---

[23] From the booklet of the cd John Zorn, Spillane 1988.

Composition

"I am devoted to my work. So my children are the compositions, the records, the performances. And my family? That's the musical community. And that's why it's not an unusual thing for me to create the Stone or create Tzadik. That's what a father would do to put clothes on the back of their children or make sure they get to a good school or protect them if they're being bullied."[24]

Zorn is an artist who seems to live his life as a continuum where life and art coexist at every moment, and who is proud to declare that he hasn't the need of a private life. In some respects, he remembers Frank Zappa who lived his life solely for the music by adjusting his biological cycle for his work needs and who was continuously composing, in an almost compulsive way, only after a while to re-invent his sketches and notes into new compositions using also pieces and cuts of the recordings made during his live tours.

Zorn has always stated that he has two fundamental interests: cinema and music, and having to choose, he preferred music because of the financial difficulties (fund-raising), the long times of accomplishment, and his poor propensity to promote himself in small circles and in the right environments[25].

---

[24] John Zorn The Working Man by Bill Milkowki
https://jazztimes.com/features/john-zorn-the-working-man/

[25] "I went into music because to do film you need a lot of money and have to spend a lot of time schmoozing and fund-raising. I have friends who make films. They come to me and say, "We want you to do the music;' and I say, "Great, where's the tape?" And they say, "Oh no, we're fund-raising now. It's going to be three years before ... " This is what it's like! I'm not good at going to parties. Music was something that I could do with a pencil and a piece of paper. But film is still an important influence on what I do, and a constant companion. I can't write music unless a movie is on in the background."Ann McCutchan, The Muse That Sings, pag. 162.

Zorn studied at the United Nations School in New York, a private school where he had Leonardo Balada as a composition teacher, who assigned him as his the first task to write a guitar piece[26]. He then moved to St. Louis for a year and a half at Webster College where he discovered the music of the Association for the Advancement of Creative Musicians in Chicago, Anthony Braxton's music, Leo Smith, and the ideas of musicians such as Oliver Lake and Julius Hemphill, and where he studied with Ken Stallings.

"That music touched me directly because of its energy, its spontaneity. It also brought a lot of things together for me. I'd been improvising, but without knowing it was improvising. I'd been thinking, "What I'm doing is not really music because it's not composed." But when I heard this music that used improvisation and composition, real music by respected people, it made me feel that what I was doing made sense."[27]

Jazz listening and in particular the album "For Alto" by Anthony Braxton stroke him deeply, giving him the creative energies he was looking for to elaborate something different from the excessive intellectualism of classical and contemporary music, while maintaining its structural complexity. [28]

These dichotomies between jazz and classical music, between the desire for an ordered structure and the freedom of improvisation pushed him to look for a new path, something that could also help him to overcome those impasses generated by the random systems used by Cage: "It

---

[26] William Duckworth "Talking Music: Conversations With John Cage, Philip Glass, Laurie Anderson, And 5 Generations Of American Experimental Composers" Da Capo Press, 1999 pag. 448.

[27] The Muse that Sings: Composers Speak about the Creative Process, Ann McCutchan, pag 162.

[28] William Duckworth "Talking Music: Conversations With John Cage, Philip Glass, Laurie Anderson, And 5 Generations Of American Experimental Composers" Da Capo Press, 1999 pag. 452.

didnt'make sense to me that Cage could put a few squirrels on a page and give it to a musician, and they would go and play the piece – be up there, pretty much improvising – and say it was John Cage's piece"[29]

The first results are improvised structures, series of instructions where there were carefully marked times, notes, something that Zorn called "statues, these little events" [30].

Zorn began to write constantly following the inspiration whenever it arrived and composed "sound blocks", archiving them neatly into cards that can be retrieved and used when it comes to the need to create a new piece. This method gave its fruits in particular with the Spillane's cd:

"Because I write in moments, in disparate sound blocks, I sometimes find it convenient to store these "events" on filing cards so they can be sorted and ordered with minimum effort. After choosing a subject, in this case the work of Mickey Spillane, I research it in detail: I read books and articles, look at films, TV shows, and photo files, listen to related recordings. etc. Then, drawing upon all of these sources, I write down individual ideas and images on filing cards.

For this piece, each card relates to some aspect of Spillane's work, his world, his characters, his ideology. Sometimes I wrote out only sounds: "Opening scream. Route 66 intro starting with a high hat, then piano, strings, harp." Other times I thought of a scene from a movie like "Year of the Dragon", and I wrote: "Scene of the crime # 1- high harp harmonics, basses and trombone drone, guitar sonorities, sounds of water dripping and narration on top." That image had its origins in the scene where Mickey Rourke, who plays a Polish detective in Chinatown, goes down into the bean sprout cellar and discovers the body. It's an image that

---

[29] William Duckworth "Talking Music: Conversations With John Cage, Philip Glass, Laurie Anderson, And 5 Generations Of American Experimental Composers" Da Capo Press, 1999 pag. 454.

[30] William Duckworth "Talking Music: Conversations With John Cage, Philip Glass, Laurie Anderson, And 5 Generations Of American Experimental Composers" Da Capo Press, 1999 pag. 460.

stayed in my mind, and I wanted to include it in Spillane. So I scored it the way I would have done it if I had written the music for that film.
Sorting the filing cards, putting them in the perfect order, is one of the toughest jobs and it usually takes months. Picking the right band is essential because often just one person can make or break a piece. I set up the overall arc, but there's a real give and take with the musicians in the studio."[31]

"The file cards are the score."[32]

An interesting definition of music block could be taken by the book "A Thousand Plateaus" written by Gilles Deleuze and Felix Guattari: "We have tried to define in the case of Western music (although the other musical traditions confront an analogous problem, under different conditions, to which they find different solutions) a block of becoming at the level of expression, or a block of expression: this block of becoming rests on transversals that continually escape from the coordinates or punctual systems functioning as musical codes at a given moment. It is obvious that there is a block of content corresponding to this block of expression."[33]

Their example for such a story maker is Pierre Boulez who they regard as a radical historian for his raids in the history of Western music and at the same time as a composer able to move between "smooth space" and "striated space" : "Pierre Boulez was the first to develop a set of simple oppositions and complex differences, as well as reciprocal nonsymmetrical correlations, between smooth and striated space. He created these concepts and words in the field of music, defining them on

---

[31] From the booklet of the cd John Zorn, Spillane 1987.
[32] William Duckworth "Talking Music: Conversations With John Cage, Philip Glass, Laurie Anderson, And 5 Generations Of American Experimental Composers" Da Capo Press, 1999 pag. 468.
[33] Gilles Deleuze e Felix Guattari, A Thousand Plateaus, pag 299 http://projectlamar.com/media/A-Thousand-Plateaus.pdf

several levels precisely in order to account for the abstract distinction at the same time as the concrete mixes. In the simplest terms, Boulez says that in a smooth space-time one occupies without counting, whereas in a striated space-time one counts in order to occupy. He makes palpable or perceptible the difference between nonmetric and metric multiplicities, directional and dimensional spaces. He renders them sonorous or musical. Undoubtedly, his personal work is composed of these relations, created or recreated musically."[34]

For these two philosophers, the distinction between striated and smooth space in the music field suggests an interesting definition of composition and improvisation: "...the striated is that which fixed and variable elements intertwines together, producing an order and succession of distinct forms, and organizes horizontal melodic lines and vertical harmonic planes. The smooth one is the continuous variation, continuous development of form; it is the fusion of harmony and melody in favor of the production of properly rythmic values, the pure act of the drawing of a diagonal across, the vertical and the horizontal."[35]

What Deleuze and Guattari describe here sounds more like a non-idiomatic improvisational form (to quote Derek Bailey) than those Boulez's meticulous and total control compositions, but they point to a disjoint form of block composition that show a surprising kinship to Zorn's method.

Zorn's particular method, as he has often said in his interviews, is based on his huge passion for cinema and freak movies.

Many of the composers he admires, Ennio Morricone, Carl Stalling and Bernard Herrmann in particular, have worked almost exclusively on soundtracks for popular films and cartoons and their sound blocks emerge in the context of the development of mood changes for the same soundtracks. In the record "Filmworks 1986-1990", first chapter of a

---

[34] Gilles Deleuze e Felix Guattari, A Thousand Plateaus, pag 477
http://projectlamar.com/media/A-Thousand-Plateaus.pdf
[35] Gilles Deleuze e Felix Guattari, A Thousand Plateaus, pag 478
http://projectlamar.com/media/A-Thousand-Plateaus.pdf

series of 25 cds dedicated to movies' soundtracks, for example he assembled from three different films a series of blocks based on different kinds of compositions.[36] But Zorn's methods of composing, as we will see talking about records like Spillane, Godard, The Bribe, Radio and Torture Garden, involves gender changes within the same compositions. The use and abuse of fast changing gender blocks to disturb the lazy and 'domesticated' listener can be also found, for example, in Zorn's arrangement of "Hard Plains Drifter," a composition, or rather a series of compositions, made for avant-garde guitarist Bill Frisell.[37] The piece played by Frisell's quartet (cello, electric guitar, electric bass, percussion) moves suddenly within thirty-six blocks between twelve different keys, numerous rhythms and instrumental combinations (three, duets, solos) between R & B, psychedelic, contemporary music, reggae, hardcore, free-form shouts and Morriconian quotes.

Spillane looks like a more easily "metabolizable" job than Zorn's other things, the atmosphere that you can breath here is far more "orderly", as long as it can be considered, after so many years, still an avant-garde record. Its jazz/blues/chamber music melodies tuned by short gangster/noir flavor sketches is lucid and accessible to any listener who has a minimum of confidence with jazz and noir movies, and the extreme clarity with which this work is presented and can be listened to in relation to previous works characterized by a much more hermetic nature.

The long suite that gives the title to the album therefore features a series of "audition scenes" that consistently follow masterpieces such as "The Big Gundown" and anticipate all the cd series dedicated to Filmworks, as well as it prepares the ground for that power group that Naked City was.

---

[36] You can read about this record in the essay "8 Zorn and 1/2" by Paolo Chang in John Zorn Filmworks.

[37] You can listen to "Hard Plains Drifter," in Bill Frisell's record "Before We Were Born", 1989, Elektra/Asylum/Nonesuch Records. This passage has a subtitle: "As I take my last breath and the noose grows tight, the incredible events of the past three days flash before my eyes." and offers a broad range of stylistic experiments, from bluegrass to noise.

Spillane is, in fact, a well-calibrated collage of "local" jazz fragments, with a double bass and piano atmosphere, moving between screams, debris, blues, free jazz sparks, contemporary splinters: all the Zorn's musical Gomi. Every piece refers to some specific aspect of Spillane's work, his world, his characters, his ideology. Sorting all the file cards, putting them in the perfect order to create a meaningful structure that reveals a function, a project below, and making a group of musicians specially selected for performing it...this is a perfect example of compositional challenge for Zorn:

"Sometimes I bring in written music and I run it down to the players, layering and molding it as it is being played. Other times I'll simply say something like, "Anthony, play some cheesy cocktail piano." Or, "Bill, go and improvise My Gun Is Quick" (an early Mickey Spillane novel), and we'll do take after take until we're all happy that every note is perfect."[38]

John Zorn's music involves the creation of a new form of attention and listening: his stated goal is to shock the listener by causing awareness, activating his "political participation in listening.". His music produces palpable effects, stimulating a form of action, awakening: it activates the listener in a way that a lot of conventional and commercial music that cares for a consolatory or anesthetic role does not. But in doing this, Zorn realizes this affect, ironically exploiting, overturning, and exploding conventions and trite forms, known and worn out by so-called "commercial music."

"I think it's an important thing for a musician to have an overview, something that remains consistent throughout your whole life. You have one basic idea, one basic way of looking at the world, one basic way of putting music together. I developed mine very early on the idea of working with blocks. At first maybe the blocks were more like just blocks of sound...noisy improvisational statements, but eventually it came back

---

[38] From the booklet of the cd John Zorn, Spillane 1987.

to using genre as musical notes and moving these blocks of genre around."³⁹

The musical form itself, as it is linked to the sphere of production and social function, and to the artistic-aesthetic convention, provides a possible key to the interpretation of the social and aesthetic dialectics spheres, as well as it allows rapid incursion (and criticism) within the problems of postmodern methodological practices. Music, as Jacques Attali wrote in his beautiful book, "Noise: The Political Economy of Music," manifests its true nature as a "instrument of understanding", as a "new theoretical form" to investigate the dynamics of social structures. Music, as Attali explains, can offer a vital conjunction, fully realized between theoretical and practical, a theoretical form to be connected to a formal practice. But if for Attali, this vision moves on a clearly utopian character, the contrast between the creativity of the artist and the ardor created by the structure massed by society, two cultural themes that Adorno liked very much, the "novelty" and the "originality" of Zorn's music is based precisely on his refusal to accept both the original and the new as valid categories of artistic expression, within the compositional sphere and performance.

Zorn's music policy and his emotional thrust emerge from within the formal manifestations of his genre and form's parodies, his postmodernism and technocratically saturated musicality, outlining a significant political stream that runs through the flattening of musical genres, the renunciation of the idea that see the composer as a deus ex machina, a collective musical structure, a liberating noise vision, and the ransom of the consumerism logic of the music industry.

The genre's concept was often referred to as an anathematism by post-modernist aesthetic practice, particularly towards its post-structuralist manifestations: the disappearance of barriers between genres has, after all, been a major concern for many contemporary writers, painters and musicians. But this disappearance makes the "genericism" concept even

---

[39] "Zorn on Zorn." Downbeat 59.3 (March 1992).

more relevant, since the "genre itself" is located in a so negative way at the starting point for this practice. It is like if Postmodernism tried to define what he refuses by appropriating indiscriminately of other genres, without distinguishing between cultural and popular.

Kevin McNeilly in his essay "Ugly Beauty: John Zorn and the Politics of Postmodern Music" suggests an interesting comparison between John Cage's Roaratorio, his "drama" Oscar winner for radio, and John Zorn's Spillane music.[40]

McNeilly talks about Cage's "composition" as a sixteen-track sound collage, based on a James Joyce's Finnegans Wake elaborated by Cage through a series of random operations, made in a postmodern attempt to free himself, as he himself states in an interview published with the score, from melody, harmony, counterpoint and any musical theory. Cage creates music that sounds free from codified and institutionalized music, mixing togheter environmental sounds, traditional Irish music, sound effects ranging from bells and thunders, laughters and dialogues. The finished product is a panorama of decent sounds and unmoved human activity that is constantly changing.

For McNeilly, instead, Zorn's Spillane, like Cage's Roaratorio, is a genres' collage, also based on a derivative text: Mike Hammer's crime novels. This contrast between the two compositions not only indicates, for McNeill, their divergent aesthetics but also their opposite political positions: Cage, for example, appropriates and transforms a rather exclusive and "difficult" text by James Joyce, Zorn uses a parody of cut and paste of a noir pulp fiction as the basis for his work.

Cage's work begins in a soft way, with the voice that sounds like liturgical, while Zorn's piece begins with a cry that sends pure anguish and fear. Where Cage's noises blend into a melodious soundscape, Zorn's blocks blend one against each other and threatening to break from one moment to the next while each of the musicians plays their parts and their musical parodies, in combination or in opposition to each others. The

---

[40] "Ugly Beauty: John Zorn and the Politics of Postmodern Music" by Kevin McNeilly http://pmc.iath.virginia.edu/text-only/issue.195/mcneilly.195

piece of Cage is synchronous, deep, and, also considering the mix of constantly changing sounds, extensively static; Zorn's work by contrast is straightforward, immediate and extremely dynamic. Zorn's music is mimicked to its "subject": we travel through the soundscape inside Mike Hammer's mind. Cage rejects the set of possible camouflage connections, preferring not to add sound effects suitable to Joyce's prose, but creating a sense of harmony through the production of "simultaneous layers of sound and meanings.
Although I admire McNeilly's rigorous approach and his postmodern vision of Spillane's music, I believe that John Zorn's vision should be understood in a broader way, his approach seems to me very different to Cage's, and seems to imply the intensive use of complex conceptual maps.

"For me the music that I make, the music of every composer, must be living music, music which express what I have learned, what I'm thinkingand how I feel and because of this I am undertaking continual research by listening, reading, watching films, trying to have new experiences to see things from different points of view."[41]

Please note that in the beautiful booklet accompanying "Godard/Spillane"'s cd (where there is a wonderful remastering of the suite published in 1985), Zorn attributes the invention of the "file card" method to his attendance to Richard Foreman's theater:

"The "file card" process developed at least in part from techiniques learned while observing director Richard Foreman's rehearsal methods in the mid '70. His theatre at 491 Brodway was a world into itself. It was there he would get together with actors five nights a week, working out every small staging detail by proceeding through the script one page at time, moving on only when all the desired elements where in perfect

---

[41] John Zorn: Itinerari Oltre Il Suono Materiali Sonori Edizione Musicali, 1998 pag.17.

alignment. Although fool proof this time consuming and costly process was a luxury completely out of my reach until 1984, when David Breskin and the Shifting Foundation awarded me a small grant enabling me to go into the recording studio. The result was Godard and later Spillane."

Zorn adds more explicit descriptions of his method in the same booklet:

"When a single composition contains noises, guided improvisation, written passages and a variety of genre s and unnotable musical shapes, the problem of unit becomes particularly compelling. Unit in a composition means that each and every moment has a reason for being there, and that every sound can be explained within a system. Using a dramatic subject (Godard, Spillane, Duras, Duchamp, Genet) as a unifying device was a revelation. It insures that all musical moments, regardless of form or content, will be held together by relating in some way to the subject's life or work. File cards are a convenient and versatile method of storing ideas. They we re used by film directors such as Hitchcock, Welles, Lang and Lynch. A compulsive list-maker, I began using this method as far back as high school and it informed the creation of many of my works, from the "visual music" of the Theatre of Musical Optics to my arrangements of Morricone and Kurt Weill in 1983. This system was eventually expanded into what has be come known as my file card compositions, of which Godard and Spillane are two of the first and purest examples. Beginning with an intense period of research, reading books, listening to music and watching films related to the chosen subject musical and dramaticide as were jotted down on file cards. These cards were then sifted through, ordered, and fleshed out with the aid of detailed written passages, melodies, fragments, and orchestrational ideas. The band was then chosen and taken into the recording studio."

In his book "John Zorn's tradition and transgression" John Bracket quotes Rene T.Coulombe who described Spillane as a 'landmark postmodern piece'[42], Zorn instead talks about it in these terms:

"Spillane has a unity in the sense that each element deals with some aspect of Mickey Spillane's world. But in terms of sound and pitches, what's going on there? I use maybe six recurrent themes that come back and forth in different ways, and one set of chords which is reused again and again. You try to give a composition a coherent sound, the way Varese used three pitches for Octandre, or the way Carter uses intervals."

In addition to the above techniques, Zorn also uses alternative solutions and compositional strategies that allow him to keep together varied and different pieces, such as adapting, changing, and incorporating music from other composers into his work. This is the case, for example, he gives us an example of how he uses his "Gomi" and different materials taken by Boulez Le Marteau sans Maitre in his record "Elegy":

"I used the score the way Schoenberg would use a twelve-tone row or a serial box. I used it as a point of departure. Sometimes I would reverse pitch sequences; sometimes I would use every other pitch from the viola part and give it to the flute; sometimes I would take [a] rhythm from one instrument and pitches from another and put them together .... I'll circle certain areas that I like and reuse this material in a myrhid of ways. It's never a case where I'll just take the whole bar; it's more like this is just raw material that I'm using-this scale, this set, this multiphonic, etc., etc. It's incredibly organic; it makes so much sense, it blows my mind."[43]

Now we can examine another directly related record to the cinema and

---

[42] Postmodern Polyamory or Postcolonial Challenge? Cornershop in Dialogue from East, to West, to East... Postmodernism Music/Postmodern Thought. Joseph Auner and Judith Lochead, eds. (New York: Routledge, 2002) pp. 177-193.

[43] John Lowell Brackett "John Zorn: tradition and transgression", Indiana University Press, 2008 pag xiv.

built with this compositional technique: "The Bribe". Written for the same radio drama by Terry O'Reilly, this record is considered by Zorn himself the "Spillane"'s sequel, which for atmospheres, organic and recording settings, is nothing but a possible variation on that subject. The only significant difference is that "The Bribe" anticipates another fundamental evolution of Zornian poetry, which will explode with the foundation of the Naked City group: compression. After finishing the half an hour long clips of cinematic music, the Naked City will offer the same dizzying mounting in minimal sound ranges ranging from about ten seconds to couple of minutes, spraying the vinyl facades in dozens and dozens of these ephemeral eyelashes, in which (as Alberto Pezzotta notes in the fundamental volume on Zorn, "Sonora - Itineraries Over Sound", edited by Materiali Sonori in 1998), the brevity of the track is directly proportional to the speed with which the musical scenario changes.

The Naked City were a band formed by John Zorn (sax, various screams), Fred Frith (bass), Bill Frisell (guitar) and Joey Baron (drum) with the addition to the noisy and dadaist voice by Yamatsuka Eye, already with The Hanatarashi (noise generators like Einsterzunde Neubaten) and Boredoms, speed metal\free jazz band founded by guitarist Seiichi Yamamoto. Right away with their first "Naked City" record released for Nonesuch Records, they immediately set a style difficult to frame because they include free jazz, grindcore, country, swing, ambient, cartoon and B-series movies music in a seemingly chaotic and casual magma sound.

Some jazz critics, disgusted by the chaotic and adrenaline scum, suggested to file ridiculously this band among metal alternative groups, nothing more fake. The Naked City have always been distinguished for being able to create their own autonomous genre, a sort of ordered, technical, fast or melodic chaos, depending on the context, which has been able to overcome happily all these years becoming a milestone for avant-garde musicians.

"The music I wrote for Naked City is the kinds of music that gets better the more is played. I wanted to improve the quality of my live performances and using the same musicians served precisely this end. The Naked City project (which, compared with to the completely improvised ones, is based on composition) was to see how many kind of music cam be made with the same ensamble, to write very different things for the same group. The problem with naked City was that I had these five musicians as a starting point, a reference point, them alone, every time, exceptional improvisers always on the look out for new sonorities, I tried to make use of their abilities to the full by working very hard, pushing very hard until it was truly possibile to go in any and every direction."[44]

The group released seven records that describe a complex and increasingly tearing path in which Zorn and the musicians work togehter - or it would be more correct to say "cope together" - to push the boundaries of compositional and improvisation structures further, without foreclosures or prejudices of any kinds. The emphasis is both on lightning executions and on the frenetic and apparently disenchanted mounting, where innumerable forms of sonic aggression and violence coexist. In this Zorn's jump cut, the File Cards are ideally torn into tiny pieces that give rise to a crazy mosaic of microtracks where there is room for everything but with a short available time for each "shred": a dozen seconds can be more than enough to bring even the most beautiful of the phrases to life and die, and then to follow to the next mini-composition. Naked City's records covers "talk" about a sordid and sick world, starting with the photo of the assassin appearing on their debut album[45], while the covers for Naked City's subsequent works will host brutal photos of

---

[44] John Zorn: Itinerari Oltre Il Suono Materiali Sonori Edizione Musicali, 1998 pag.22.

[45] It's a black and white photo made by the great Weegee, who in the 1940s published a book called Naked City, containing photos depicting the violent, squalid, miserable or perverse side, perhaps in such a human, New York.

tortures or extreme sado-masochism.[46]
The perfect element and sum of the maximum compression capacity of information and music genres is "Torture Garden". The music and the cover of this record, which portrays images from a sado-maso movie, are the cause of the divorce between Zorn and Nonesuch Records. The record is produced by the independent Swiss record company HotHat and marks the beginning of Zorn's stubborn rejection of any contact with journalists and music critics: violent references to the hard core and metal scene divide critics and the public. "Torture Garden" immediately became a record that is loved or hated. No compromise.

"With all due respect, the critics understand nothing, absolutely nothing of what is going on stage, particulary where hardcore is concerned. In any case it is always a problem to do with musicians. There are some who play the same old clichés because, for example, they want to be considered jazz musicians,and this could seem to be the right thing... furthermore from such a position they can get status, money, fame. There are others, hardcore ones, who play even in minor bands, who go on stage because they love music, and they are exceptional, people who are really truly receptive with whom I have often played and have chosen because I admire what they do, what they manage to give and in them I see the chance all the same to open music up, to keep it a living form."[47]

Torture garden: clumsy aggression of a generation of extreme extraction, neurotic swing, expanded on 42 tracks of 30-40 seconds (from a minimum of 8 "(Hammerhead) to a maximum of 18" (Osaka Bondage)), one skinned grind at the Scum\From Enslavement To Obliteration, of the earliest and primitive Napalm Death by Lee Dorrian\Mick Harris duo, a

---

[46] About Zorn's iconography I suggest you to read "From the fantastic to the dangerous real" in the book John Zorn Tradition and transgression" by John Brackett.
[47] John Zorn: Itinerari Oltre Il Suono Materiali Sonori Edizione Musicali, 1998 pag.16.

hysterical mood that traversed a trance of absolute no-sound control. Sound and mental destabilization?
I don't think so. Zorn and his mates knew (and know) very well what they did (and do). I have read numerous criticisms and reviews that talked abouth them (in positive and negative) and about free improvisation. None of this. No Improvisation. Everything in this record has been prepared, composed and written with a composing line featuring a well-defined jazz\fusion\swing characteristic on a delusive and strict grind\core, devastated by the inahuman voice (or kyai) by Yamatsuka Eye, a true grind pioneer. Alberto Pezzotta in his essay "Velocità e Citazione"[48] gives a detailed and complete analysis of how the 41 seconds of NewJersey Scum Swamp track were made, tracking 24 music fragments, 24 frames of a movie soundtrack, mounted on the sequence of a simply frenetic and paroxysmal rhythm, with the addition of pure noise interventions to add a sense of disorder and apparent discontinuity.
Pezzotta's musical analysis clearly reveals some of Zorn's musical editing features: heterogeneous and distinct themes and genres are contrasted, triturated and mixed with each other while maintaining their distinctive features. The principle is simple and a clear post-modernist matrix: mixing with each other by equating them and reducing them to decontestualized melodies, rhythm and noise, "high" and "low" music, more or less easily recognizable and undistinguishable sounds and noises. The effects of this sonic centrifuge are quite obvious: the listener is forced to work hard as well as to remain as suspended while awaiting the immediate and inevitable accompaniment noise. However, in Torture Garden, the fragmentation process is accelerated to the maximum speed. There is also a precise reference to splatter titles and images, as we can easily see reading the following titles: Thrash Jazz Assassin, Blood Duster, Shangkuan Ling-Feng, Perfume of a Critic's Burning, Blunt Instrument, Sack of Shit, New Jersey Scum Swamp, Cairo Chop Shop, Victims of Torture and Fuck the Facts.

---

[48] "John Zorn: Itinerari Oltre Il Suono Materiali Sonori Edizione Musicali, 1998" pag. 29.

Torture Garden's centrifuge, the maximum exemplification of a medium beyond which it was impossible to push forward, allows to highlight another important aspect of his composition/assembly mechanisms: the speed and the ability to compress information.

"When a single composition contains noises, grunted improvisations, written passages and a variety of genres an unnotable musical shapes, the problem of UNITY become particulary compelling. UNITY in a composition means that each every moment has a reason for being there, and that every sound can be explained within a system."[49]

The hyperbolic mounting speed of heterogeneous soundtracks on the model of cartoon music, advertising and music videos is one of the fundamental problems that we meet when we try to decode Zorn's compositions at least in his earliest times: how does he manage all the connections? In other words, how does Zorn integrate, connect, merge in a coherent way the mass of his manifold insights, elements and relationships that he elaborates with the file cards' method.

One of the features of his music, highlighted by the seven records made with Naked City, is always a form of informative bulimia: Zorn doesn't filter, doesn't select or decides what to put on the first sight, what to blur. Simply he compresses everything. In this sense, his idea of the composer abdicates with one of his fundamental prerogatives: to select what to represent his own creative world (and the outside world). If we imagine Zorn's music as a network of connections, the composer becomes one of the crucial knot of this net. A network mesh that delivers information, with the added bonus of increasing compression, the complexity of living and feeling, saturate the limited listening ability of the listener, already distracted by other media.

The Zornian composer solves this limit by working through the reduction of his musical ideas, influences and quotations to short, subliminal suggestions of an episodic character, assembling them in a highly-

---

[49] From the booklet of the cd "Godard/Spillane".

contrasted, seemingly illogical, cinematic editing. The advantage of this mechanism is to allow the listener to be able to activate his attention in his most congenial moments, based on his own experience, tradition and taste, without thereby running the risk of losing through the fragmentation of listening to the sense of the whole work. There is no longer a need for rigorous interpretation, as in the musical malestroom the interpretative tools are subtracted. With each new listening you can redefine the patterns, create a new tradition, discover new elements by (re)connecting them to create something new while keeping the music alive.

Jokingly, Zorn says that his music is suitable for impatient people, as crowded with a large amount of information that changes very fast: the listener, if he finds anything he doesn't like, just wait for ten seconds until he turns into something different. But Zorn's speed is something more, it's a combining, centrifugal force with which he better joins together his sound blocks, so that the "protruding" sounds encourage the interlock between the storage cards where stores his short pieces. But for Zorn, speed is a reading key, a paraphrase of our society, of our world:

"Still, you've got to realize that speed is taking over the world. Look at the kids growing up with computers and video games-which are ten times faster than the pinball machines we used to play. There's an essential something that young musicians have, something you can lose touch with as you get older. I love bands like Husker Du, Metallica, Black Flag, Die Kreuzen. Speed bands, thrash bands ... it's a whole new way of thinking, of living. And we've got to keep up with it. I'll probably die trying."[50]

Is this Futurism? The same transition to modernity pushes music, popular and not, to a higher rhythm speed (let's think about techno and its subgenres), but above all to the mixing of a discontinuous / syncopated performance and new sound texture, musical plots which are entrusted with the task of evoking the new civilization of machines and

---

[50] From the booklet of the cd "Spillane".

communication The same television language has evolved into shapes that don't allow for breaks and reflections. Speed of language imposes rhythms that are out of touch with the types of traditional communication, just think of the speed of dictation achieved in television news or advertising of medicines. Eight syllables per second seem to have become the ideal frontier for a response that does not annoy a TV spectator accustomed to switching channels at a frequency of every 12-15 seconds.[51]

If the first work of the Naked City was an almost cinematic journey in a nocturnal New York, with noir atmospheres and marked by the vices and virtues of an incessant pulsating heart, and Grand Guignol and Torture Garden definitively opened the door to a revolutionary and fragmentary compositional form's conception, based on music blocks as well as sonic and bloodthirsty sounds defined by critics such as jazzcore, "Radio" represents the ideal sequel to the first homonymous album.

Here the space for improvisation is reduced to the minimum necessary to make the overall listening accessible to a much larger circle than usual: only short sound interstices, no lengthy avant-garde suite, the package includes nineteen well-developed and autonomous songs with an average length of three minutes, for a total duration that is close to the total time. The album is ideally subdivided into two different parts. The first nine songs are in the form of the pure fun, with few or no concessions to metal funambolisms, and indeed developed on relaxed and disassembled registers, easy listening and assimilation. Then, slowly as the CD progresses, the tones begin to blur, to change: they swear, become more dry and ferruginous, grow in intensity and power. In the original notes accompanying the first edition of the Zorn record, it compiles a precise list of music/composers/groups/genres that would be the basis of each song and there are no surprises: for example, the "Outsider" where we find the mentioned Ruins, Booker T. and the MG'se Colin Wilson, "Terkmani Teepee", who spins between them surfing, reggae and bossa citing the Accüsed, the Meters and Yakuza Zankoku Hiroku, the new

---

[51] Stefano Pivato "Il Secolo del rumore" Il Molino 2011.

wave of "Razorwire", where Frisell argues his great guitar skills, and where Tony Williams' Lifetime is quoted. Beautiful "Krazy Kat" is a jumble of short musical strokes that are different from each other, which passes continuously from operetta to cartoon, jazz, metal, country, clear cartoonistic tribute to Carl Stalling and Igor Stravinsky.

Carl Stalling

Carl Stalling seems to be a real holy guardian for Zorn. We can find Starling widely quoted in the Spillane's booklet: "Cartoon music is a very strong influence on the way I put that apart the disparate elements of my pieces.", but his (and also Stravinsky's) musical approach seems to represent an effective solution to the problem of the creative longevity of an artist raised in Godard / Spillane's cd leaflet[52], a problem brilliantly resolved, according to Zorn himself, through the composition block method.
But who was Carl Stalling? Born in the small town of Lexington, Missouri, the young Stalling got his first contact with music playing an old toy piano. In 1903, at the age of five, he saw "the Great Train Robbery" and from that moment on he was determined as his own words show "to be close to the movie world in every way and at all cost ". Seven years later, he would become the local pianist of his city's film productions, a very old factory with only one designer, in which Stalling also played during film changes. In the early 1920s, Stalling directed his orchestra and improvise on the organ at Iris Theater in Kansas City where he met Walt Disney who decided to give him two pieces for two short clips featuring Mickey Mouse, a new character who had only appeared in a previous cartoon.
In Hollywood, in the newly-built Disney studio, Stalling gave birth to a real cinematic revolution, giving the breath of life to inanimate cartoon characters through his music. In this sense Stalling was one of the most

---

[52] "An important secret to longevity as a composeris in setting yourself new challanges and finding new ways to overcome them."

revolutionary and visionary authors in the American music, especially if one considers his temporal conception. Following the logical view of the actions on screen rather than the traditional rules of the musical metric form (development, theme, and variations, etc.), Stalling succeeded in creating a composition entirely based on the flow of images on the screen, unprecedented in the History of music.

At first listening, Stalling's immense musical talent hits the traumatic capacity (resumed and amplified by Zorn himself) to resume and mix together diverse and heterogeneous musical elements by interrupting the music flow with continuous variations and changes through a constant kaleidoscopic transformations of different styles, shapes, melodies, quotes, or footage of piano pieces for the Kansas City's mute films, elevating them to the value of a science with Disney and to the value of an artistic representation with Warner Bros.

Stalling worked in a period governed by American conservative impressionism, pervaded by the will to search for new sound sources and Stalling was no doubt one of the most extreme composers of that period. A pioneer who showed us kindly, using the innocence and lightness of the cartoons, a new universe full of all kind of goodies: from all possible change of humor to the slimmest musical journey to the most exaggerated and upsetting transformations. A world where Willie the Coyote chases to defeat the diabolical Road Runner by challenging all the laws of physics, where Bugs Bunny terrorizes poor Taddeo with surreal sadism and neurotic Daffy Dug tries to capture Speedy Gonzales, the fastest Mechico mouse.

His music, which for years we have listened to without knowing it in the background of the masterpieces of Tex Avery, Chuck Jones and other Warner Bros's animators, presents musical and conceptual elements that are simply disconcerting for the years in which they were elaborated.

For example, concrete noises (a clear anticipation of what will come next) appears to be used inside the narration, like animals' sounds used like real tools to emphasize particular atmospheres and free from the usual rigid structures of the traditional scores.

As John Zorn remembers, he graduated with Stalling's thesis, the 1930s and 1940s were crucial for American music history: jazz, swing, hillibilly, the first distant etnomusicological discoveries (base of exotic music) and a handful of American composers looking for new ways in opposition to the solutions adopted by European colleagues: Partch, Antheil, Nancarrow, Cage and Varese.[53]
Stalling is signaled for his will to include all kinds of music, one at a time or all together, whenever necessary, giving him an opening, a non-hierarchical musical point of view, typical of today's younger composers, but really rare in his own time. All musical genres are of equal importance, nobody is better off than others and with Stalling everyone is embraced, mixed and diversified in a pattern similar to Burrough's cuts or Godard's 60's movies, rather than every other events that took place during the '40s.
Zorn would obviously omnify Stalling in his composition Road Runner, composed for Guy Klucevsek's accordion.[54]

Ennio Morricone

As a movie lover, Zorn could not meet the music and the ideas of Ennio Morricone. An extremely prolific and original composer, featuring impressive stylistic versatility, in more than sixty years of career, Morricone has worked for cinema, TV, radio, theater, advertising and pop music (also as arranger). Morricone is also the author of choral compositions, chamber music, symphonic works for solo or orchestra, contemporary works. He has traveled to the boundless territories of classical music of all times, he has written pop, rock, jazz and world music scores, and has often experienced, at his own risk and danger, the expressive possibilities of instruments that had never entered in a

---

[53] Notes on the booklet of the cd The Carl Stalling Project: Music From Warner Brothers Cartoons 1936-1958 (1990).
[54] The score can be viewed in the book: "John Zorn: Itinerari Oltre Il Suono Materiali Sonori Edizione Musicali, 1998" pagg. XXIV e XXV.

classical orchestra, such as the electric guitar or the italian "scacciapensieri"[55], succeeding in affirming his own inexhaustible talent and conquering the public of the whole world.

Morricone gave to John Zorn (who went to meet him while the Roman composer was working on orchestration for Brian De Palma's movie, The Untouchables) the basic lesson: "Do not think about the movie, think about the music of the movie."

Thanks to the insistence of producer Yale Evelev and the confidence gained and deserved with the rework of the music by Monk before and Kurt Weill later, Zorn in 1985 releases one of his most important records: The Big Gundown, where he proceeds in an elaborate re-reading of Morricone's sountracks.

For Zorn, the challenge was too tempting to let go: finally he was given the chance to get out of the restricted circle of underground music worshipers, relying on one hand on the full support of the record company, on the other hand a name of a sure recall such as Morricone and finally the full chances of choosing the musicians with whom to create the music. In practice, the full control over the whole project and full freedom of action.

John Zorn's clever and brave arrangements work on these soundtracks with the clear intent of breaking and opening their structures. Zorn doesn't give any embellishments to original music, but rather engages into a combat, a hard interaction at the limit of the neurosis with Morricone's music sometimes with jolly and joking tones, sometimes with silly and skeptical ones. Musical parody is one of the characteristics of Zorn's music of those periods (80s), but here he goes beyond, his music crosses the theme of the Rawhide show to get to the Big Gundown. Zorn zoomed on Burt Bacharach's suggestions of the "Duck, You Suckers!" soundtrack and slammed the gentle, "Sean, Sean...Sean, Sean" with a more effervescent "shoop...shoop". If Morricone's "Milano Odea" runs almost mechanically, Zorn carefully dismantles the mechanism and redesigns it so that the individual parts are not properly welded together.

---

[55] Jew's harp.

In "Duck, You Suckers!" the Japanese shakuhachi and Tsugani shamisen point out the Kurosawa Yojimbo as a sort of ur-text at the base of Sergio Leone's cinema, while the "American" harmonica in "Once Upon a Time in America" strides with the most "Italian" accordion.

Sometimes Zorn intensifies the aggressiveness already expressed by Morricone in his compositions. In the original version of "Metamorfosi" (from the soundtrack of "La Classe Operaria Va in Paradiso"), shaggy and sharp shriek, suggesting the Gothic interior of a factory or slaughterhouse, move togheter with mocked chamber music and spectral laments, such as a dark symphony, following the method of composition that Zorn will deepen with Spillane. Zorn's adaptation is beyond any abrasive way, with unhappy rhythms and groans of horrifying death: as if workers were awakened to hell. For the "Battle of Algiers," Zorn doubles Morricone's martial rhythm and undermines his heroic theme with anxious bouts of orchestrated noise, whistles, cavalry charges and shouts. In the soundtrack of "Peur sur la Ville" by Henri Verneuil (the film is the story of a psychopath who calls women on the phone and then strokes them), an initially melancholy and sweet airy is gradually blocked by sequences of dissonants and twisted gugles, such as those produced by an orchestra while agreeing before a concert. What Morricone develops horizontally, Zorn puts in practice squeesing his maniacally compressed guitars, saxophones and rumors into a heavy metal hold.

Amazing bunches of sounds also galvanize the ambitious suite that Morricone composed for Sergio Collima's "The Big Gundown", translated by Zorn in his own idioms. The inspiration for this piece comes from a dream. Zorn initially thought of a version with Brazilian salsa added with a layer of surf guitars to add some flavor. Before recording, however, Zorn had his first dream of his life, which was pure music. He woke up in the middle of the night and wrote the music he had just heard, that not only became the track's introduction but to the whole record: a Brazilian batucada ensemble is certainly unscrupulous by massacring phrases taken by Beethoven Fur Elise with the addition of peper guitar noises. The result is not only a hardening of the original version but a further increase in the sense of frustration and threat already expressed by the main theme, which is reduced to spasmodic and almost desperate fragments.

An original composition of the New York saxophonist, which amplifies the experimental charge expressed in the passages of the Roman master, finds space in this record, which is a sure sign of the commitment he has poured into this project, namely "Tre nel 5000", its original composition that in a sense "vaporises" the ideas and styles of Morricone to create a song that cites everything and nothing, with continuous references that continue to escape the listener, Zorn transcends Morricone, realizing that there is nothing innovative In re-propagating the avant-garde ideas of another generation and therefore prefer rather to draw on the vitality of Morricone's music by placing it at the center of each performance, reworking and re-synthesizing according to their own sensibilities and experiences.

Improvisation

Like composition, improvisation is one of the key elements of Zorn's music organization. Between 1974 and 1992, Zorn has produced about thirty special pieces known as Game Pieces, which represent his personal answer to the main problem behind the improvised techniques: how to give an organization to the most radical and informal improvisation. For organization I mean a macro structure that would be flexible enough not to cling creativity, while at the same time providing soft but defined rules that effectively coordinates a group of improvisers. Taking inspiration from experimental music, theories of computational games, and ultimately by the studies about social conventions, Zorn has conceived these compositions not in terms of metrics, language, instrumentation, or notation, but simply with rules that set up games' scenarios for a group of improvisers, whose inventiveness and capabilities need to be constantly under pressure, challenged by the constraints defined by the composition's rules, which, indeed, form the composition itself. The composer limits himself to providing a set of behavioral norms that musicians must adhere to during improvisation, leaving them completely free to follow their own inspiration.
This musical corpus is part of the Game Pieces, a composition/execution system that combines teachings and instances previously developed by John Cage, Earle Brown, Karlheinz Stockhausen and Cornelius Cardew. The stated objective is twofold: inserting musicians into a complex system based on flexible compositional formats and at the same time limiting the scope of performers/interpreters within a precise time limit.
To do this Zorn notes his ideas on a blackboard, slowly proceeds by assembling and carefully smoothing the various elements, trying to represent a world within each piece. All of these Game Pieces then began to live their lives regardless of whether or not Zorn was the conductor of the ensemble performing them, becoming his most performing pieces all over the world: Australia, Japan, United States, Great Britain, Germany.

Despite this success, however, Zorn has radically refused to publish the rules underlying these pieces, preferring to explain himself during the rehearsals as part of an oral tradition.

The rules vary considerably from one game to another and may have to do with limitations of the musician's speech to five possible sounds as in Hockey or with an intricate communication system between the musician who had an intuition, the conductor that registers and relaunches and the whole group that has to follow it, as in Cobra.

Other composers tried to collaborate with improvisers or, more often, with musicians who, although inexperienced, were required to improvise. Christian Wolff (in his Prose Collection), Robert Ashley (in "word scores" at the beginning of the 60s) and Karlheinz Stockhausen, among others, formulated what Stockhausen himself called "intuitive music." Unfortunately, most of these pieces are fairly simplistic to be "classified" as more closer to the Fluxus collective, a phenomenon of the 60s that included participants such as Yoko Ono, Nam June Paik and LaMonte Young.

Significant and above all innovative is the new attitude towards composition (from premeditated to indeterminued) and the transformation of the role of the performer, who is no more the impeccable interpreter of a score, as the score is no longer thought in terms of a language that pairs in almost behavioral symbols and answers, but as a code that must be made to speak and act by the performers, creative accomplices of the composer. This is John Cage's example.

In 1938, Cage has the intuition of taking an ordinary piano, inserting elements of metal, plastic, wood and fabric between the strings of the instrument creating his "prepared" piano. Cage's goal was to achieve a sound result no longer linked to the expressive force of the composer, but to a causal and virtually limitless sound alteration, using the case to achieve the indeterminacy of performance by removing any volunteer/subjective act from the composition. Cage went even further by adopting even a compositional method based on the launch of a set of Chinese dices: each launch, according to a pre-organized index system, refers back to notes, volume, intensity, dynamics, etc.

Although Cage defines his music as casual and not improvised, these practices, which intend to introduce indefinite elements into the compositions, seem at first sight close to the borders of improvisation.

Another method adopted by Cage for his music by change was the graphic notation, which was successfully adopted in 1958's Fontana Mix, where the score is made up by a series of transparent sheets of partial annotations to be superimposed on one to an others randomly, generating a different map each time. Similar techniques of graphic notation had already been adopted by Satie, Ives and Cowell, and more radically by Morton Feldman for "Projection 1 for solo cello" composed in 1950, whose score, like other Feldman's compositions, looks like an abstract painting. "The Piano and Orchestra Concert" (1957/58) is Cage's masterpiece of indeterminacy, as it doesn't have an actual conductor, whose role is purely theatrical, so that every musician plays his part independently and without any coordination with the others. This Concerto has no binding score, and the pages contain mostly lines and dots and a series of instructions that govern how the performer can make decisions (in his reflections on musical composition, Cage explains how the "case" can not simply happen: it's necessary to elaborate a method in which the stochastic element has a role to play). This concert has a mobile structure, being all the decisions about the sounds and their succession delegated, through experimental suggestions on the actions to be performed, by the composer to the performers.

Ironically, in his final act to leave everything to chance, denying the individuality of the performer and considering it secondary to the role of composer and fate, Cage ended up being on the same positions as his old teacher, Mr. Schoenberg, who considered interpretation as a kind of improvisation, making every effort to overcome this possibility.

In fact, Cage's incursions into the world of casualty had begun a bit earlier. In the late 40s and early 50s, before joining IRCAM, he consolidated a strong friendship with Pierre Boulez. Cage and Boulez were both lonely and struggling avant-gardists. At that time Boulez with his total serialism offered absolute control over music by pre-determining all aspects of a musical piece, not just frequencies and notes, but also rhythm and dynamics. But serialism and casualty are two faces of the same coin and it has often been said that the music produced by randomness and totally predetermined music sounds very similar and equally arbitrary, Boulez himself recognized later that his 'automatic' music actually generated a sort of anthropic anarchy, a kind of "chance by the back door".

Otherwise in 1951, Boulez wrote, probably after having realized how much his and Cages's ideas were in opposition to each other: "The only thing, forgive me, which I am not happy about, is the method of absolute chance (by tossing the coins). On the contrary, I believe that chance must be extremely controlled...I am a little afraid of what is called 'automatic writing', for most of the time it is chiefly a lack of control..."[56]

The European avangarde has always had a more "cautious" attitude toward "music by changes" than the counterpart on the other side of the Atlantic Ocean. Boulez and Stockhausen developed methods of generating indefinite factors, but rigorously within well-defined parameters, such as the 'mobile form' developed by Ives and Cowell.

Also Karlheinz Stockhausen, with "Klavierstuck XI", his 1956's piece where nineteen fragments scattered in a large score are ordered according to various possibilities that the performer has to choose (so that the attack and the order of the fragments can be considered in many ways improvised), or Morton Feldman with "Intersection 3", and partly also Luciano Berio with his "Sequenza"series, have cultivated the idea of an undetermined performance so different from the usual composition, where ever larger portions of sound material are under performer's control with margins for improvised conduction (in this sense Stockhausen could talk about his music as a "permanent genesis"). The composer merely provides information on the initial conditions and how to conclude the work, and the performers have the power to collaborate by making decisions within a field of possibilities, and collaborating with

---

[56] Undercurrents: The Hidden Wiring of Modern Music, pag 212.

the author in completing the musical action. Similar to the case of "Intensitat", for ensemble, by Aus den sieben Tagen (1968), Stockhausen has no score, not even the initial and predefined configuration, but only a text that invites each musician to play a single sound with such dedication from alert the heat radiating, then asking the musician to support this sound for as long as possible. No score, no indication about the coordination of musicians, only this invitation.

Clarinetist Anthony Pay said in this regard: "He invites you, for example, to play in the rhythm of the molecules that constitute your body, or in the rhythm of the universe." There is an anecdote about it, it seems that the second violin asked for the German composer: "Herr Stockhausen, how do I know when I will be playing in the rhythm of the universe?" and Stockhausen would reply with a smile, 'I'll let you know' and he's probably still waiting for a nod on his head[57]. However, by 1970, Stockhausen had returned to exact notation, his most radical work already completed.

Xenakis's 'stochastic composition' was not really chance. But he did write three pieces based on mathematical game theory: "Duet" (1958-59), "Stratégíe" (1962) and "Unaia Agon" (1972-82). Duel is a game between two orchestras, with the conductors as active contestants. Xenakis drew comparisons with competitive situations in folk and jazz. Nouritza Matossian suggests that the psychological roots of his interest was the feeling that his own life had been saved in Athens, during the wartime Nazi occupation, only by chance.

A real radical, no more part of the academy than the same Cage, was the self-taught Argentinian composer Mauricio Kagel, a person who had a great influence on Zorn. Influenced by Dada and Surrealism, as well as by Cage, his "Match" (1964), is a composition that features a musical contest between two rival violoncellists, with a percussionist in the role of referee. As Cage, Kagel rejects the pure improvisation doctrine, "if indeed this ever existed." What is realy important in his work is "strict composition with elements that are not pure themselves": rigorous

---

[57] Derek Bailey, Improvisation, pag. 72.

composition with elements that are not pure. In "Exotica" performers must try to master non-western instruments to themselves strangers, Kagel exploits that, when the sound of the instrument is unknown to the performer, this also involves the introduction of an unexpected unforeseeable element: every instrument is a bit 'aleatory' at the beginning. In a way that recalls the roots of the division between Boulez and Cage, Kagel commented on his "Saint Bach Passion" that "totally planned things [as in serialism] and totally arbitrary ones have a similar piece".

At the end, however, all of this sound like rhetoric. It's like if the musical criticism about "contemporary" improvisation tries to make us believe that this corresponds to a pure academic discipline of real-time composition, born through intrinsic tension to the development of modern classical music, as if composers, frustrated in their expressive will, and induced to react to some formidable excesses of serial music (which sometimes became a true compositional orthodoxy), had come to something new and self-contained.

Terms like "random", "indeterminate" seem to have been coined to circumvent the world "improvisation", which the same composers seem to have a crazy fear.

On this aspect Zorn seems to have very clear ideas:

"For many years, Cage was very resistant to improvisation. It's interesting that the word "improvisation" was very dirty in the classical music world of the 60s. It was almost as if it was an insult to the composer if someone used the word "improvisation." I can understand why composers at that *time* felt compelled to justify their work with intellectual systems and words such as "aleatoric," "intuitive," and "indeterminate." They were trying to justify to the critical community that this was not "improvised music"-music that the performers were making up as they went along-but music that was truly envisioned by a musical mind and then passed down to the performers."[58]

---

[58] Christoph Cox, Daniel Warner; Audio Culture:Readings in Modern Music;

What many of these composers failed was not to understand that this new compositional form requires not only new forms of notation, but also new aspects in the ability of a musician. While many European-class musicians can be competent in the area of contemporary music, they haven't necessarily the sensitivity to improvise an intrinsically coherent and inventive music piece.[59]
When Earle Brown or Morton Feldman created sheet music that required melodic inventions (or graphic interpretations), these were interpreted by "conventional" "new music" professionals referring to their usual practices so that music had a tendency to play, paradoxically, more ultra-controlled than spontaneous. Conversely, when composers such as Frederic Rzewski, Alvin Curran, or Elliott Schwartz require improvisation in one of their pieces, the improvisers were generally Steve Lacy, Evan Parker, or Marion Brown, and so their music sounds different.

At the beginning of his career, Zorn found a big problem: it seemed that most of the world's population did not want to take it seriously, suffering from "unspeakable abuse" by both critics and the public. Maybe the reason was that he played duck's calls immersed in water bowls?
"Right, well, people look at me and I'm playing duck calls all laid out on a table.... And at this point in my development, a lot of the work that I'm doing is involving the duck calls and the sounds I'm getting from them in the water. And I don't play the saxophone as much as I used to in concert, maybe only 15 percent of the time. Everything else is with mouthpieces and pieces of the horns laid out on this table. And it's developed over

---

Continuum International Publishing Group, 2004 - pag. 197.

[59] "One of the problems that both Earle Brown and John Cage came up against was a certain friction and resistance from classical players to work in those kinds of open contexts. Cage perversely thrived on that friction between what *he* wanted and what *they* didn't want to do. There was a drama about it. And he could kind of sit there and laugh about it in some Zen-like fashion. I don't think Earle had that same kind of sense of humor. I think he was a little more tormented by it. "Christoph Cox, Daniel Warner, 2004 pag. 197.

eight years or something."[60]

The first use of one of these calls is on Eugene Chadbourne's "The English Channel" (1979). From then on, the use increases with the purchase of new calls in specialized stores.[61]

The Parachute Years

In his interview with Ann McCutchan in the book "The Muse That Sings: Composers Speak About the Creative Process" Zorn declares that the inspiration for the Game Pieces came from "In C" by Terry Riley[62]. Please, don't misunderstand the confrontation with Terry Riley's "In C". "In C" is a piece composed of "fifty-three separate phrase doodles - average length, 10 notes- which are required reading for each of the eleven instrumentalists who partecipate in the piece"[63]. There is no conductor and interpreters can play every phrase as many times they like to with the only rule that they can't repeat a phrase already made. The piece is considered completed when the eleventh musician completes the

---

[60] Interview with Bill Milkowsky del 02/11/1983 pubblicata su Rockers, Jazzbos & Visionaries.

[61] "The first one ever was a Greenhead duck call that Mark Miller, the drummer, gave to me. And I used that on Eugene's recording, *The English Channel,* from 1979. And from then on it just grew and grew. It got to a point where I would go into a hunting store and they didn't even want me in the store any more. At first I tried the duck calls in the store with my mouthpieces to see if they fit. Then they wouldn't let me try them anymore so I'd just go in and buy their stock. Sometimes I play them on their own, sometimes I attach them to my horns. But then, the guys in the hunting stores, man, they didn't wanna know about me." Bill Milkowsky, Rockers, Jazzbos & Visionaries, pag. 224.

[62] "I look at it as a later In C [Terry Riley's seminal minimalist work]: some'" thing that is fun to play, relatively easy, written on one sheet of paper." Ann McCutchan "The Muse That Sings: Composers Speak About the Creative Process".

[63] Glenn Gould, The Glenn Gould Reader, pag 226.

53th phrase, leaving the performers free time, with a duration between 40 to 90 minutes. The tone of this piece, as indicated in the title, is C. Its structure is therefore radically different from Cobra with which it shares maybe a certain "participatory" and as ironically tells Glenn Gould "Music like In C requires instruction rather than education, and that's an altogether more subjective matter."[64]

"I wanted to have happen weren't happening. I'd wonder, "Why aren't people leaving more silences?" So I'd write a piece for improvisers that inherently had a lot of silences. Or, "Why doesn't everybody, all of a sudden, change at one time?" So then I'd create a little system and write a piece involving that."[65]

Zorn has composed about 25-30 game pieces. The first ten of them explored in a very specific way several improvisation management issues: "There was a piece about putting different genres of music on top of one another in an Ivesian way, and a piece about concentrating improvisations into short statements, so that every player thinks very hard about every note."[66] All these pieces involve the musicians in the compositional process and must be performed in a precise time span.

"The game pieces worked because I was collaborating with improvisers who had developed very personal languages, and I could harness those languages in ways that made the players feel they were creating and participating. In these pieces, they were not being told what to do. You don't tell a great improviser what to do, they're going to get bored right away."[67]

The problem that Zorn faces seems to be the one that always accompanies those who play improvised music: to endure more than a

---

[64] Glenn Gould, The Glenn Gould Reader, pag 227.
[65] Ann McCutchan "The Muse That Sings: Composers Speak About the Creative Process pag.163.
[66] Ann McCutchan "The Muse That Sings: Composers Speak About the Creative Process pag.163.
[67] Ann McCutchan "The Muse That Sings: Composers Speak About the Creative Process pag.163.

few minutes and to work with an ensemble a form that is based on improvisation must contain a simply miraculous sequence of extemporaneous inventions, which can not be prepared at a table, or a compositional structure which is not at the same time noticeable or overweight.

Musicians involved in the process become the crucial factor, a fact that Zorn co-operates with other musicians and leaders, primarily Miles Davis: "I'm writing for my group, for something Jack can do, that Chick can do, or what they want to do, what they have to do is go beyond what they think they can do, and they have to be fast. A solist is paid for it, if it does not work, I'm jamming it up like obstacles, barriers, just like in the streets, just like I do it with my trumpet."[68]

For Zorn "composition is problem solving" and improvisation is no exception. You can always tell the improvisers to play a piece using only three sounds and then incorporate this seemingly simple idea into more complex structures. Faced with such a structure a classical trained interpreter would not know how to line up, while an improviser might find the exciting challenge, knowing that it could always play an infinite number of times completely differently.

This thing has also a significant impact in terms of musical socialization, that is to say, the social construction of music, the way social relationships enter into music, intervening in the sound construction of musical events.

"Eventually in the game pieces I created sets of rules, like the rules for baseball or football, and the players would interact using those rules. If they followed the rules properly, they could create certain structures and tactics, do whatever they wanted at any time. "You don't want to play? You don't have to play. If you want to play, here's the way you go. You want to play with this person? You can do this. Some pieces are meant to be ten or fifteen minutes long; some can last a full evening or go on forever. There's no set beginning, middle, or end, but there are ending

---

[68] Hubet Soal "Miles of Jazz" in Newsweek 03/23/1979.

cues-you can call them at any time. Some pieces can be for any number of players, some are for three players, some are for any instrumentation, some for a specific instrumentation. Each game piece is like a series of toggle switches-on and off, on and off-with a very complex series of rules that make it challenging. I'll never be one of those composers who says, "OK, everybody, let's do a little piece that says 'Water.'"[69]

Cobra

Cobra is the most famous, executed and published Game Pieces. We can find four different versions on vinyl and cd. Basically, Cobra is a small company, within which every citizen, or any musician, finds or tries to find his own place. Sometimes it becomes a psychodrama where people have the power to do something. It's really interesting to see how some of them, for example, distance themselves from this power, others adapt to the situation with docility and do everything that is said to them; others still rebel and aim to dominate trying to gain control and to have more and more power. In a sense, it reflects what is commonplace in politics. This is a set of rules that all musicians must respond under the control of a master, a conductor, a bit like in the role games (to which the same title of the piece refers). It's fundamental, therefore, the contribution or rather the presence of Zorn who runs among the musicians, eliminating the distance and working with them, contrary to the usual orchestral direction expected in classical music. On the other hand in this Game Pieces you can't leave the musicians alone, they need a direction that is entrusted to the so-called "prompter". All the musicians refer to him during the performances by asking for the word (for handshake). The musician chosen by the conductor establishes an entry corresponding to a card indicating a part of the body (eyes, nose, mouth, palm, etc.). the hint shows the paper to the others. Everyone performs, according to the rules of the card shown. It goes on so until the prompter/conductor says: ok,

---

[69] The Muse that Sings: Composers Speak about the Creative Process by Ann McCutchan.

for today it's enough.

As we said, Zorn has always refused to publish a real Game Pieces' method. One of the main reasons is that Game Pieces are born in relation to specific musicians and can't be considered otherwise. Since the Game Pieces/musicians binomial is the founding element, the main value is not in the individual sound fragments, but in knowing how to create the right ensemble, and this is something that can't be schematize or standardize. Thinking about it there is just a chance to really learn something like Cobra: understanding how it works, then entering a dynamic and varied community (like that of New York musicians), gaining respect, learning its implicit rules. Although this piece contains simple rules and not pentagram notes and can potentially be executed by anyone, this is not a purely abstract composition: it was originally intended for the different languages of the new school of improvisers that in those years was forming in the East Side of Manhattan, musicians with whom Zorn had been in close interpersonal relationships for years.

Zorn was very explicit about this in Cobra's reprint notes: "To do this music properly is to do it with a community of like-minded musicians and an understanding of tactics, personal dynamics, instrumentation, aesthetics and group chemistry. It's about cooperation, interaction, checks and balances, tension and release and many more elusive, ineffable things both musical and social. First and foremost it's about playing good music."

At the same time, however, he is also aware that this kind of pieces and their musical structures can live their own life and be replicated even without his presence: "These pieces can go anywhere anyone wants to take them, and since they live in the underground as part of an oral/aural tradition, this becomes one of the dangers as well as part of the fun. Nevertheless there can be no such thing as a definitive version and I'm sometimes pleasantly surprised by tapes of renegades versions I receive in the mail. As more and more musicians become interested in playing these pieces and my control over individual performances becomes more and more tenuous, it is my hope that this new series of cds documenting my game pieces will show a few of the possibilities and some intended directions."

Perhaps the best Cobra's definition belongs to Guy Klucevsek who played in the first version of this piece: "In 1984, I heard John Zorn for the first time at New Music America/Hartford, performing his game piece, Rugby. This performance challenged every idea I ever had about ensemble playing: here was a situation where every decision in the piece was being made by the performers, guided by a set of instructions provided by Zorn. I was so excited by what I heard and saw that I ran up to Zorn on stage, introduced myself, and told him if he ever needed an accordion player in a future project, I wanted to do it. The next year, Zorn took me up on my offer by inviting me to join the Cobra big band. With Cobra, Zorn was able to do for the '80's what In C did for the 60's: create a classic piece for open instrumentation for performers who wanted to be part of the creative process of realizing a piece. Cobra codifies just about every aspect of free improvisation: instructions are provided which enable individual ensemble members to determine orchestration, dynamics, density, types of material, endings, even the ability to call back events which happened earlier in the performance ("memory systems"). And, in a quintessentially American move, Zorn provides "guerrilla systems" for those independents who don't like taking instructions from anyone."[70]

The entry of Klucevsek into the Cobra ensemble had for him other positive effects on his music and his career as a musician: "The Cobra band was made-up of people whom I was meeting for the first time: Elliott Sharp, Bill Frisell, Bobby Previte, Wayne Horvitz, Zeena Parkins, Carol Emanuel, Arto Lindsay, Christian Marclay, and Anthony Coleman. I had no contact whatsoever with the free improv scene before, but I have since collaborated on numerous projects with many of these same people."[71]

---

[70] Guy Klucevsek "Accordion Misdemeanors: A Musical Reminiscence" http://www.ksanti.net/free-reed/essays/misdemeanors.html

[71] Guy Klucevsek "Accordion Misdemeanors: A Musical Reminiscence" http://www.ksanti.net/free-reed/essays/misdemeanors.html

One of the things that distinguish Cobra from other aleatory systems used in music is that in the only "score" available for this piece, placed inside the cd Cobra Vol. 2 published in 2002, Zorn didn't show any "traditional" musical notation. It's like if Zorn wanted to abdicate any control of the sonic origin of music in favor of Cobra band's improvisers, limiting himself to adopt a form of "remote control" that allows him to handle changes in the "programming" of the passage, always following the rules set by him, but without predetermining what will be played.

Cobra can share a spiritual/intellectual relationship with Brown or Feldman's work where music is understood as a "potential environment" or as a live performance pieces that are essentially "activity programs" that give up each specific control in sound terms and just define the chances of choice, the fields of activity, and the inability to predict the end result. There are, instead, substantial, fundamental, essential differences, not based on what Zorn wants to play but on who is participating and how he inspires them to built a "creative interaction"[72].

I think that Cobra is based on a kind of implicit oxymoron: musician's complete freedom within demanding "game" rules. Whatever these rules define, they don't represent a limitation or a direction for individual activity, but a social condition that makes musicians a community itself and requires a thorough awareness of the ways of interaction, patterns of behavior and the results of the their actions. In my point of view, it doesn't appear to be an attempt to limit self-expression, is not intended to create the independence of individual musical parts (as in some contemporary music claiming to want to marry "freedom") but a interdependence between the parties based on the independence of thought

---

[72] "...it's kind of a loose system that permits improvisers to interrelate and react to each other in different ways.
And you as conductor control it by...
Zorn: I don't control it at all. It's all up to the musicians in the group. They control it. They make all the cues, and they tell me what they want, and then I act like a mirroring device so that everyone can see what the cues are."
http://browbeat.com/browbeat01/zorn.htm

and the choices made by musicians, creating a complex web of relationships in which personal dynamics are in the hands of the participants.

Being based on indeterminate rules, Cobra assumes the character of those who participate it. Without fixed perimeters, it's in a continuous state of becoming, exploiting forms of simultaneity that transform relational flows into musical structures generated by the ensemble who work on the rules and process defined by Zorn. Each performance will undoubtedly be drastically different in terms of sound and structures depending on how the participants will bring their own private perceptions, past experiences, instrumental techniques, and interpersonal attitudes to tackle and manage the opportunities offered by the game piece.

This difference is also the result of a stylistic evolution of the musicians themselves. Two generations have already passed since the early improvisers of the 50s and today's musicians have developed a much more versatile approach to the cornucapia of styles available to them, from classic to pop. The result of the work of these people is not, as you could expect, chaos or total anarchy, but instead, democracy, interactivity and interdependence. And despite the continuous and rapid changes in textures, time, and temperament we can see an order, a spontaneous and sometimes ironic organization within the resulting chaotic musical logic.

The starting idea is based on cartoon music and in Cobra there is a specific command that musicians can impart to the group - Zorn calls it "cartoon trade" - which is the ideal link that support Zorn's work on the different fronts of the game theories and kinematic music.

To get an idea of how a game piece works, when inside Cobra's collective creative flow a single musician intends to propose a cartoon trade, he hasn't to do anything else, once caught the prompter's attention (Zorn or who for him), pointing the eye and raising a finger. When registered and evaluated the request, the prompter raises (from a series of posters placed in the center of the semicircle in which the musicians are arranged), the signal corresponding to the musician's wish - in this case an orange colored card "CT" writing - thus communicating it to the whole group.

From the moment the prompter lowers the card, the command becomes operative and all the musicians will come up in a skirmish of noxiously assembled noises as long as someone will not make a further signal to the prompter by manipulating the creative process.

At the end it is always Zorn, the composer, to have the last word: "But above all, COBRA is a musical experience words cannot convey blah blah blah. Listen, just listen, and you're liable to find yourself lost in the magic of the game, and the music."

THE BOOK OF HEADS

John Zorn and Agatha Christie

What do a New York-based saxophonist/composer/improviser with a somewhat difficult character and the queen of the British detective novel have in common? Apparently nothing. It is sincerely difficult to imagine two such different and distant personalities. But I think we can find something: the originality of the narrative mechanism. In 1926 Mrs. Christie published what is now considered to be one of her most famous and at the same time the most controversial novels: "The Murder of Roger Ackroyd". This adventure of Hercule Poirot is set in a quiet village in the English countryside, Kingston Abbot, whose doctor, Dr Sheppard is also the book's narrator. The original feature of this novel is that the narrator, in the end, also turns out to be the murderer. This factual originality guaranteed the work a huge success and made it one of the most famous novels in the history of detective literature. It has in fact been the subject of numerous studies in the body of human sciences that have taken its cue to analyze theoretical problems raised by the singularity of its constraints.[73]

In this second part of the book I will initially use this text to better analyze another one: John Zorn's Book of Heads, 35 guitar studies characterized by another narrative expedient: the absence of a musical score annotated as a classical, traditional music score. Both of these texts are characterized by an aesthetic beauty in the construction of their narrative artifice and it will be my attention to use Agatha Christie's novel to better analyze the characteristics of Zorn's work, in particular one of the most interesting aspects of the BOH: the complexity of its interpretation.

Just as "The Murder of Roger Ackroyd" can be reread by legitimately

---

[73] The book has been commented on by Roland Barthes, Gerard Genette, Algirdas Julien Greimas and Umberto Eco, as well as by writers such as Raymond Chandler and Alain Robbe-Grillet.

questioning the outcome of the investigation made by Hercule Poirot[74], every interpretation of the text of John Zorn can be legitimately exposed to new rereadings. In this exam I tried to stick as closely as possible to a form linked to rigor and the desire to follow a logic as clear and flawless as possible, avoiding as much as possible the risk of elaborating a delusional musical reading myself, following a path similar to that of the detective novel, a path that consists in the meticulous search for clues, to interpret the facts and to put together all the deductions in a coherent and harmonious narrative building. This will not exclude some possible twists and turns, in line with the detective literary tradition, even if I am not Belgian, I don't wear mustaches and, above all, I am not Poirot. The best thing, of course, would be that the reader himself had time to read Agatha Christie's novel. But, perhaps, aware of the difficulties of satisfying this request, a small summary of the book would not be a bad thing. The novel is set in the village of King's Abbot, where its most illustrious and wealthy citizen, Roger Ackroyd, is found murdered by a Tunisian dagger he owns, in his studio. Hercule Poirot, a brilliant and bizarre investigator who retired incognito in that country, is commissioned by his granddaughter, Flora Ackroyd, to discover the culprit. Whoever it is. The suspects include Flora herself, her mother Cecil Ackroyd (Roger's sister-in-law), Major Blunt (a famous hunter), Geoffrey Raymond (Ackroyd's secretary), Ralph Patton (Ackroyd's penniless stepson), Parker (the butler), Ursula Bourne (maid of the Ackroy house and secret wife of Ralph Patton). The book is narrated in first person by Dr. Sheppard, who also performs the role of assistant to Poirot (role normally played by Captain Hastings), and ends with an unexpected twist: Poirot, after having cleared all the suspects, demonstrates the guilt of Dr. Sheppard. The doctor's account, initially born as an attempt to describe Poirot's failure in the hunt for the murderer, eventually turns into a confession that ends with the narrator's announcement of suicide.

Agatha Christie in her novels has always known how to exploit an incredible masking ability. In all her plots and also in the relationship

---

[74] As Pierre Bayard did in his brilliant book "Who killed Roger Ackroyd?".

between her stories and the reader, she has always known how to reinterpret the same crime plot by deceiving the reader himself with subtle efficacy. This sophisticated writer has been able to express this aspect of the unconscious without requiring the deciphering of hidden senses, but inventing from time to time different mechanisms that aim to prevent the reader from perceiving the truth. And while exercising this mimetic art, she shows the other side of her mimicry: the police investigation, the interpretation and the movement through which a sense is produced.

I want to work on this mimicry and this productions of meaning, starting from detective literature and what it can bring: not the unveiling of mysterious latent contents but allowing, thanks to the variety and complexity of the models it proposes, to reflect on the creative phenomena and on the ability to face them. All theoretical literature on the detective crime novel is dominated by a principle of dissimulation[75] that Agatha Christie seems to have brought to perfection, a principle that can be divided into two rules. The first is that the truth must remain hidden throughout all the book: the detective novel makes sense only if the truth is not revealed before the end of the text. The second is an aspect of the same principle: although hidden, the truth must be accessible to the reader and even highlighted. If the truth would be linked to elements that the reader has not available it would not be gender-compliant. This principle was applied in a masterly way in EA Poe's "The Stolen Letter" and one can read the entire work of Agatha Christie as the rigorous and systematic application of this principle: in her novels all possible combinations, that allow you to play with that dual aspect and to prevent the reader from accessing the truth while offering it to his gaze, have been experimented with great rigor and success.

BOH represent something "anomalous" in the context of the more consolidated and traditional classical compositional structures. They represent an alternative solution in which different factors come together

---

[75] This fundamental principle of the detective novel was conceptualized by S: S: Van Dine in an article that appeared in 1928 in "American Magazine".

to form an integrated and solid structure. Something very similar happens to the abandonment of the third-person narrative in the Christie's novels: the composer ceases to be the "deus ex machina", the main responsible for the final result. If in classical music we normally face the traditional separation between the figure of the composer and that of the interpreter, in BOH this social, cultural, economic and musical distinction ceases to have a clear boundary. Everything becomes much more nuanced. Responsibilities erode themselves, the semantic boundaries fall apart. The composer renounces the role of narrator in the third person facing a polysemic model that considerably increases the virtual number of interpretative solutions, playing a logic that foresees several different results. With BOH the interpreter goes up on the same level as the composer. Just as in the Christie's novel, the narrator and the guilty get confused, so it happens in John Zorn's BOH, creating a broader narrative. I wonder if Christie's novel and Zorn's compositions focus us more on the means of concealing the truth or on the difficulty of establishing a sense, because the variety and complexity of the proposed solutions risk to create a polysemy's model in which each element, tipped an infinite number of times, becomes doubtful. This polysemy is first and foremost tangible, since this novel and these studies explicitly propose a whole series of readings, but also a virtual polysemy to the extent that the combinatorial possibilities obtainable overwhelm the whole text as a reserve of hypotheses, valid until when the final solution allows one of them to impose itself on the others. The problem is therefore to know how this virtual polysemy does not end up creating undecidability, frustrating interpretative models. A conceptual labyrinth in which even Borges could get lost.

In this book I will try to follow the same investigative pattern followed by Hercule Poirot during his investigation. In the case of "The Murder of Roger Ackroyd" we find the traditional structure of the detective story, which by contrast supports a brilliant detective and a stupid policeman which leads to two different investigations with two different conclusions. While the police conduct classic reasoning that identifies a plausibile murderer, Hercule Poirot advances on his own, using unpredictable logical procedures that lead to a completely unexpected culprit. The two paths are the result of two different logical procedures that lead to two completely different interpretations of the facts. The investigation by Inspector Raglan, carried out in the light of the sun, leads him to suspect Ralph Patton: he hasn't an alibi, he is full of debts, heir to the deceased's assets and after the murder he disappears, becoming the ideal suspect. Poirot's inquiry, and his interpretation of the facts, proceed in the shadows, showing only some incomprehensible clues, until the surprising final revelation. If it is true that Poirot, like the police, evaluates all the clues available to him, his attention focuses on a number of secondary aspects to which he returns carefully throughout the story and which will be the basis of his conclusions: the phone call announcing to Sheppard the death of Acroyd, the chair moved in the murder room, the Patton's shoes. These three elements lead him to the unexpected accusatory conclusion: Doctor Sheppard is the culprit. I will try to apply the same relentless logic and the same positivist confidence shown by Christie also in the case of the BOH: we will analyze the clues left on the field by John Zorn and his associates and we will see how their analysis will lead us to a series of possible solutions available to the interpreter who had decided to play them.

The first clues come directly from the CD "John Zorn Book of Heads" released for Tzadik in 1995. The black obi, which has always accompanied, with Japanese elegance and design, the releases of the independent New York record company quotes verbatim:

"Toy ballons, talking dolls, mbira keys, wet fingers whops, whisks, knocks, multiple harmonics: these 35 études for solo guitar, composed in 1978 for Eugene Chadbourne, give a new meaning to the word 'virtuous'. Masterfully performed by Marc Ribot."[76]

---

[76] Notes from the obi of the cd "John Zorn The Book of Heads", Tzadik, 1995.

The obi already gives indications on the nature of the "instruments" to be used during the execution of the 35 studies composed by Zorn, in addition it clearly indicates to whom they were dedicated and composed: the guitarist Eugene Chadbourne, who in those years (1978) was a prominent element within the independent music scene. Zorn goes straight to the point when, in the notes written in the small leaflet that accompanies the CD, he says:

"Composed in the summer of 1978 at a time when I was spending almost every day at the Metropolitan Museum of Art in search of inspiration, this music was originally written for and is dedicated to guitarist Eugene Chadbourne. Meant to GAS him, and to stretch his already prodigious virtuosity to even wilder extremes, many of the extended techniques used here (toy balloons, talking dolls, mbira keys, wet finger whoops) were learned from him and were an integral part of his improvisational language at that time. Others are standard to contemporary classical guitar notation (body knocks, whisks, bowing, multiple harmonics) and still others were the product of my own sick imagination (playing with pencils, rice, pulling strings out of the bridge notch)."[77]

Zorn also says:

"Condensed from over 80(!) original pieces (a composition device I have often utilized - it's better to have 1 strong piece than 5 weak ones), these 35 études each define their own musical universe with an improvisational language distinct unto themselves, yet still are unified into a single compositional vision. With each pieces I've tried to stretch the capabilities of the guitar in various directions relating to harmonic voicings, sound aggregates, textures, simultaneity and finger control. Perhaps these musical miniatures will one day be used to help introduce creative techniques and effects, teach improvisational skills, or even just fun as part of the standard guitar cannon."

---

[77] http://www.tzadik.com/index.php?catalog=7009

These few notes already give us some important indications on the period of realization of these pieces, where they were composed, to whom and for whom they were designed, but above all they give us a setting, a context in which to be able to insert and enhance them.

Twenty years later Zorn will return to the topic on the occasion of the second edition of BOH, also on Tzadik, played by James Moore. In the booklet that accompanies this second CD, Zorn tells us how, at the age of 10 in 1964, he became interested in the guitar and how instead of being interested in what was proposed to him by his teacher, he was more attracted "in seeing how many different sounds I could coax out of the instrument". Zorn also tells how the rich music and art scene in the East Village was created in the second half of the 70s and his meeting in 1976 with Eugene Chadbourne. Zorn adds more details about the birth of the studies:

"The BOH was written for Pops to play solo (after watching Tim Corey in Kubrick's The Killing, Eugen and I called each other "Pops"[78] and I worked on it from 1976-1978. It incorporated all the crazy sounds I had developed on the instrument up to that tome, some techniques that were central to Chadbourne's style of the late '70s (ballons, whoops, mbira keys) and musical ideas from a variety of improvising guitarists – Frith, Sharrock, Bailey, Kaiser, Duck Baker, Davey Willimas, etc, etc. Everything I knew about the guitar was reduced and distilled, filtered throught my bizarre compositional vision and molded into these 35 brief etudes for a solo guitar."[79] The first performance (premiere) took place in 1976 at the Theater of Musical Optics and then later in 1978 at one of the "Olympiad" Game Piece Festival at Studio Henry (One Morton Street)."

---

[78] I think this explains the reason for the writing Pops on the covers of the two Cds.
[79] Notes from the cd "James Moore Plays The Book Of Heads - CD and DVD of a film by Stephen Taylor", Tzadik, 2015.

The 70s

Art has always been communication. This is not a discovery[80]. Art, under the veil of the symbol and metaphor, has always transmitted the historical situation, its ideology and psychology, the mentality of the contemporary public and, in the following times, has provoked a valid reaction to understanding the point of view and the relationship with that particular work of art.

The 70s were the decade in which the potential of rock, both in terms of size and misery, came to fruition. In the 1960s, rock had evolved from a shapeless mix of various popular genres to an art form that considered itself at the same aesthetic level as poetry and classical music. The 70s saw the pulverization of rock with the birth and rapid rise of funk, glam, disco, electro, post-punk, ambient, new age, heavy metal, prog rock, punk, new wave and hip hop. We can say that since then nothing new happened in the pop music, if not some sub-genres and crossovers of those just listed. Indeed, it was also a decade characterized by the most banal and stereotyped forms of rock ever, together with some of its most deafening and experimental moments. Just mention any attribute of rock, from glam to heavy, from hard to soft, from intelligent to stupid, from ecstatic to depressing, and you can find unmatched examples in the 70s.

Maybe it was simply a natural passage in the evolution of a genre: rock was born in the early 50s, in the 70s it was in the late teens, its 20 years, the period in which experimentation and creativity often reach the climax. But there were also important political and social factors. The dreams and hopes of the 60s collapsed between 1968 and 1974 with the assassination of M.L. King and Robert Kennedy, the election (and re-election) of Richard Nixon, the escalation of the war in Indochina, the repression of the student riots in Berkley, the killing of students at Kent State University and the economic recession, that followed the increases in the price of oil decided by OPEC.

---

[80] Mario Maffi, La cultura underground II, pag 20.

The newspapers were full of violence. Ramon Navarro, Harry Partch's ancient lover, was tortured to death in his house by a gigolo determined to find the money hidden in the house, and there was no money. Richard Maxfield, author of the piece for magnetic tape "Amazing Grace" (1960) anticipating minimalism for the use of loops and samplings obtained from the voice recordings of the Reverend James G. Brodie, committed suicide by throwing himself into the void from a window in San Francisco, padded of drugs. In August 1969 Charles Manson ordered his followers a series of heinous crimes in the canyons of Los Angeles[81].

I think the rock music of the '60s came to an end with the tragic Altamont concert, where the riots caused four deaths, and an apparent period of disenchantment took over. But instead of putting an end to experimentation and creative energy, this disenchantment somehow pushed the musicians in a new, darker direction: in the early 70s there was a despair that was missing in the 60s and fed the music bringing it to new heights and new abysses.

There were also changes in the way music was listened to and played. The era of three-minute singles was over. October 31,1975 the British group "The Queen" changed the rules by publishing the single "Bohemian Rapsody", a song of almost 6 minutes accompanying it to a music video that made school and is still today considered among the most famous and most important of its kind. The era of LP's rock albums was born. The LP, a medium created by CBS in 1948 gave rock and jazz groups the freedom not only to lengthen the times, but also to conceive their music as high art.

The bands that dominated the 60s, Beatles and Rolling Stones, no longer had the scene in their hands, and dozens of other equally ambitious bands, Led Zeppelin, Pink Floyd, CSNY, Black Sabbath, Who, Jethro Tull, Doors, etc ., were vying to take their place. Rock was now free to divide into various subgenres and to expand and diversify into: hard rock and soft rock, Californian and New York rock, black rock and southern rock, heavy metal and glam.... The record majors entered a period of

---

[81] Alex Ross, Il resto è rumore, pag.789.

prolonged confusion, provoked by the unprecedented success of albums without singles, such as those of Led Zeppelin. Warner Bros and Atlantic simply decided to leave maximum creative freedom to their artists, without imposing any limitations whatsoever. And a huge number of these artists started making big bucks.

"By the '70s Jimi Hendrix and Janis Joplin were dead; Jim Morrison's death followed. Corporate rock began to grow. It wasn't until the end of the '70s that the "punk moviment" was fabricated by England's Malcom McLaren, who made it fashion. McLaren took what he saw in a few American groups – the Ramones, Richard Hell and the Voidoids, and the New York Dolls – and packaged it in the form of the Sex Pistols, whose music proclaimed anarchy and the end of rock'n'roll."[82]

Then there was the drug. The marijuana that fed the 60s was now so widespread that if you didn't smoke it you risked ending up ostracized. Heroin and cocaine made their triumphant entry in the 70s. Amphetamines, barbiturates, alcohol and acids were fearfully increased and accessible. Being a musician and not being in an altered state was so rare that it was almost unheard of. The creeping desperation of the time fueled excesses and excesses fueled despair, both stimulating an unprecedented level of unconventional creativity. This aesthetic enhanced the spontaneity and collective improvisation, the jam sessions of Jimi Hendrix, Grateful Dead, Sly And The Family Stone, Captain Beefheart and Neil Young were shining examples. Later this aesthetic will degenerate into an emptiness for its own sake, but for a few years it was supported by drugs, despair and driven by ambition. The right balance to produce masterpieces.

Barry Miles in his book "In The Seventies: Adventures in the Counter-Culture"[83] stated that the 70s were the real age of drug, rock 'n' roll and

---

[82] Kim Gordon, Is it my body? Selected Texts, Stenberg Press, 2012 pag. 98-100.
[83] Barry Miles, I Settanta, pag 206.

sex, even more than the 60s, and writing for a music magazine was like being at the center of the vortex, the drug was everywhere. All you had to do was show up at the offices of a record company at 10 am, ready to go on the bus or a limousine to a concert or a press conference where the manager was ready to offer you eloquently the cocaine tube and the spoon silver.

According to Miles, punk spread like a virus triggered by Kate Simon's photos in which Malcom McLaren, in 23/04/1976, attacked a hippy in the front row at the Sex Pistol's concert in Nashville, a perfect example of a viral pre-marketing[84]. It was an absolutely gratuitous episode of violence, triggered by Vivienne Westwood who, out of nowhere, had started to slap the girl next to her, a perfect stranger. The victim's boyfriend had protested and McLaren had come forward, followed by Johnny Rotten. Vivienne said she did it "because she was bored". Then on 20 and 21 September there was the International Punk Rock Festival at 100 clubs on Oxford Street. Despite the absence of journalists at the event, Punk and the violence surrounding it sparked a great debate, mostly in negative terms. Rock reporters finally had something to gossip and sell on. It was something obvious and new, a form of high intensity rock still in development. And if journalists targeted it, it meant that it was good for sure.

Much of the excitement of punk arose from the public, from the enthusiasm fueled by amphetamines and from creative clothing, because punks dressed to amaze. The girls wore men's shirts torn and held together by safety pins, full of band names written with a marker or ballpoint pen, and tattered fishnet stockings. Or they sported old sweaters collected in second-hands markets, torn in the right places. The black garbage bags and the transparent plastic raincoats were also very popular, the omni present pins, both in the fabric and in the flesh and later also the extreme nudism[85]. Even more important than the clothes was the make-up and the haircut, showing a marvelous creativity: geometric shapes drawn

---

[84] Barry Miles, I Settanta, pag 213.
[85] Barry Miles, I Settanta, pag 213.

on the cheeks, zeros and crosses, eyeliner in industrial quantities. Hairs were shot up and multicolored. Somebody wore a swastika to amaze, but it was exasperating.
New York was populated by a much more aggressive, detached, punk race, aware of its own badness. The London punks were far from being kind to each other, but there was a sense of belonging, of community: they were mostly proletarians. In New York, the punk scene was more than anything else the incoherent cry of anger from a lot of young bourgeois looking desperately for an identity. They were more arrogant, drugged, rude, more nihilistic and ultimately more alone.[86]
And then there was Patti Smith. April 16, 1976 Patti Smith played at the Roundhouse. His guitarist, Lenny Kaye, was the author of the famous anthology of garage groups "Nuggets", a compilation that would mark an aesthetic path in an area that did not even want to hear about aesthetics. Please note that Smith's first record, "Horses", was produced by her friend John Cale, the most musical and avant-garde in the Velvet Underground. In 1976 at the presentation of the concert at the Intercontinental Hotel in London she made a mess that went down in history: provoked by a journalist and eager for anger and malice, she jumped on a table and barked:

"I'm the Field Marshal of rock'n' roll! I'm fucking declaring war! My guitar is my machine gun! "

Too bad that, as Barry Miles pointed out, she had not yet learned to play the guitar, which until then she had used as a symbol, not as an instrument[87].
If we go back to the tensions of the 60s, their close connection with an expansive economic phase that was beginning to show the first signs of fatigue, appears to us with greater clarity. Much of the protest movement against the system stemmed from the confused feeling of threatened well-

---

[86] Barry Miles, I Settanta, pag 239.
[87] Barry Miles, I Settanta, pag 231;.

being. It was not by chance that riots started inside the petty-bourgeois class, among intellectuals and students, among those classes eternally threatened both from above and below, by the capital and the proletariat. Half classes that perceived the danger of a bottleneck, of a funnel intended to seriously affect the positions of relative tranquility, the result of a economic boom exploded in the 1950s on the push of a lightning expansion of surplus value[88].

In the 70s the term 'underground' became improper: it lost all its strictly cultural meaning, ceasing to be the distinctive term of that sector of dissent entrusted to the written word, the cinematographic image, the theatrical gesture, the graphic sign, the cultural or hippie social experiment, and expanding to embrace all that reality which for different purposes dissented from the American system and proposed new solutions and ways of struggle[89]. Culture merged, subordinating itself to politics. The underground became part of a much larger body: the "Movement". The "Movement" was the new front of dissent in the 70s: a cumbersome and protean front whose borders were the most distant and disparate instances. The geological strata of dissent exploded, shattering any tendency towards crystallization and sectorialism, and in the frenetic chaos resulting from the anarchist base it was not possible to generate the emergence of a political party.

Within 4 years (1968-1972)[90], politics reached all layers of dissent, defining a period of cross-fertilization, of axioms, of passage of elements from one sector to another, of expansion of the territories of action. The attempt in music to escape the omnivorous market, that transformed every creative input into hard cash, was symptomatic.

Art history is not an orderly progression of works that develop as a consequence of the other[91]. Underground artistic production arises from the meeting of a series of needs closely linked both to the character of the

---

[88] Mario Maffi, La cultura underground I, pag V.
[89] Mario Maffi, La cultura underground I, pag 41.
[90] Mario Maffi, La cultura underground I, pag 45.
[91] Arthur C. Danto, After the end of art, pag 28;.

counterculture and to the specific conditions in which it operates and acts on. Two interdependent floor, influencing each other. The concept of game is the main nucleus around which the whole underground revolves during the 60-70s in its social, cultural and political expressions[92]. A very particular way of creating, working, doing politics, acting in the artistic and cultural field was born: a way undoubtedly unacceptable according to the artistic and cultural academic canons at those times. Music becomes more and more the mirror of the youth world, transforming itself into its medium par excellence, more and more creative, aggressive, inventive[93]. Thanks to some avant-garde musicians such as John Cage, Molton Feldman, LaMonte Young, etc. music became the basis for certain mixed forms such as happening and as an inspiration for themes, rhythms and techniques of underground movies.

By the late 60s it was already clear that anything could become music. The history of art in the 70s was not an orderly succession of music, scores, performances, improvisations but a heterogeneous assortment of works created with various means of expression. In the 70s everything happened, and everything at the same time. We began to learn to live in pluralism. The present age, called contemporary as opposed to the modern one, is not governed by any great narrative. The great narratives, that defined traditional art first, then modern art, came to an end in the 70s, contemporary music no longer allowed to be represented by any genre of great narration. We live today in an era of great pluralism and absolute tolerance, at least in the art world and perhaps only in it. Nothing is excluded. Whatever music came from then on, it would not have benefited from the reassuring narrative frame that presented it as the next stage of an evolution.

A characteristic of the 70s is that, unlike the previous periods, they had started quietly, without slogans, without symbols, without anyone being particularly aware of what was about to happen. No manifestos, no

---

[92] Mario Maffi, La cultura underground II, pag 1.
[93] Mario Maffi, La cultura underground II, pag 7.

directives against the past[94]. In the 70s the artistic expressions of the past were not something to fight against, but something available to the artists and whatever use they wanted to make of it, describing not a style as much as a way in which the styles were used. In other words, it was a period defined by the absence of stylistic unity, or at least of a unity to be raised to criteria and to be taken as a starting point for acquiring a faculty of recognition. The conditions of a unique narrative direction failed. It was a period of information disorder, a condition of total aesthetic entropy without a univocal direction but characterized by an incredible productivity and experimentation in music, without a univocal narrative orientation. The 70s produced a paroxysm of styles, the competition between which helped to clarify that there wasn't an unique way in which a work of art had to present itself in order to differentiate itself from the past. And I think there was also a big net difference: whatever the music was, it was no longer just made to be listened to. As Cage sanctioned with his silent passage.

The 1970s saw the end of the concept of manifesto[95]. Arthur C. Danto defined the manifesto as something that circumscribes a certain type of art and style and declares it as the only one that matters. Each manifesto therefore conceived its own art in terms of a recovery narrative, a discovery or a revelation of a lost or only vaguely glimpsed truth. It was based on a philosophy of history that defined the meaning of history as a condition of soul, identified with true art. This point of view obliges to an a-historical and detached reading, identifying each specific artistic style as monochromatic, abstract to any other type, suggesting that everything else represents a form of false art. An a-historical reading, in which all artistic expressions would in fact be identical, in which all art would be abstract. Modernist art historians seem to have mysteriously endorsed this idea, because their opinions in favor of a type of art were similar to autodafè, sentences of the inquisition, almost another way of declining the logic of the manifesto, with the consequence that anyone who did not

---

[94] Arthur C. Danto, After the end of art, pag 30.
[95] Arthur C. Danto, After the end of art, pag 33.

join them had to be suppressed, like a heretic. Heresy hinders the progress of history. In terms of critical practice, the result was that if individual artistic movements didn't write their manifestos, critics arrogated to themselves the right to write for them.

Modernism was the age of manifestos[96], whose fundamental contribution was having introduced the philosophical dimension into the heart of artistic production. Accepting art as such meant accepting the philosophy that guaranteed it an artistic citizenship. The profound truth of our historical present consist in the fact that the age of manifestos ended because the premise, on which the art inspired by them was based, was philosophically indefensible. A manifesto isolates only a type of art, legitimizing it by declaring it the only and authentic form of art, as if the philosophical discovery of the ultimate truth in art were due to its movement. Until the twentieth century there was a tacit belief that a work of art was always identifiable: the philosophical problem today is to explain why something is art. Take care to the attempts to distinguish between music and noise, between dance and movement, between literature and simple writing. See the distinctions made between a traditionally conceived score and the new personal graphic writings of the composers who are contemporary to us. This does not mean that all art is the same or undifferentiatedly valid, but only that its limits and characteristics do not lie in expressing oneself in the right style or in recognizing oneself in a specific manifesto.

In "Music with Changing Parts" (1970) Philip Glass and his ensemble went beyond the duration of an hour, tracing clear modules around static harmonies[97]. Over the next four years, Glass assembled the monumental cycle "Music in Twelve Parts", with performances lasting for four hours. In this work he summarized the various methods he had developed up to that moment, he explored new rhythmic and harmonic solutions in the last two parts, he thought of a music with rapid chord changes. The starting point of Glass's musical phase was the opera "Einstein on the

---

[96] Arthur C. Danto, After the end of art, pag 29.
[97] Alex Ross, The rest is noise, pag. 550.

Beach" created between 1975 and 1976 in collaboration with Robert Wilson. After four centuries of opera history, "Einstein on the Beach" created a new type of music theater. The premiere took place in Avignon in the summer of 1976 and in November of the same year it was shown twice at the Metropolitan Opera, it was sold out, but the composer got a debt of 90,000 dollars and for a while he decided to drive his taxi again. Downtown music had entered a phase that Alex Ross defines as "grand minimalism"[98].

In the summer of 1970, Steve Reich went to Ghana to study with percussion master Gideo Alorwoye, who taught him to play the polyrhythms he had read in the writings of A.M. Jones. He returned to the USA with the need to write a more dilated type of music for a large ensemble, in which the participants could contribute with their energies to the action. The result was "Drumming", a minimalist tour de force of almost ninety minutes. In the next piece, "Music for 18 musicians", Reich added strings, woodwinds, voices and piano to create an authentic minimalist orchestra. The premiere took place on April 24, 1976 at New York's Town Hall. In the 70s, the downtown Manhattan scene reached the height of its influence. Composers from all parts of the U.S.A. arrived in the city to join it. The rents were cheap, the spaces hosting the alternative performances didn't care for artistic/aesthetic limitations, the public showed a positive attitude. Phill Niblock worked on slow glissing made of electronic sounds amplified to a crazy volume, which sounded hypnotically in the acoustics of the surrounding space with devastating power. The composer singer Meredith Monk pushed her voice to the extreme to create a sort of new Ur-folk music, a virtual language based on sensual chants.

When the Philip Glass Ensemble played "Music for changing parts" in London in 1971, Brian Eno was in the audience. He also attended the Steve Reich and Musicians concert, in 1974. Eno gained a sort of fame around 1971 by playing the keyboards and sound effects of the art rock

---

[98] Alex Ross, The rest is noise, pag.551.

band Roxy Music[99]. In "For Your Pleasure", Roxy Music's second album, Eno introduced Reichian phase shift effects, pushing minimalism into pop music. Eno letf the group to become a solo artist, an incredibly successful record producer, director of a record label, technician and sound curator and freelance composer. He diffused a new kind of music called "ambient", a music that floats on the edge of the listener's awareness, without heaviness. In 1971 also David Bowie was at Glass's London performance. In the Berlin trilogy "Station to Station", "Low" and "Heroes", Bowie abandoned the classic A-B-A pop song structure moving toward semi-minimalistic forms, characterized by rapid and curious rhythmic pulsations. Modules and cells taken from Reich and Glass appeared in the disco hits in the late 70s and then infiltrated the darker and alternative environments of techno, house and rave music. Thurston Moore and Lee Ranaldo, who played guitars in the famous post punk band Sonic Youth, authors of a new form of alternative rock, had met while playing in the electric guitar orchestra of the downtown composer Glenn Branca.

---

[99] Alex Ross, The rest is noise, pag.555.

New York, New York

BOH's history is a New York's novel: in a sense, it couldn't have happened anywhere else. New York is certainly the most mythicized, the most famous city in the United States. A city where the American Dream reaches dangerously high peaks: the city where the most legendary success joins the most ignominious failure. An attractive black hole for creatives of all kinds. A city of violent contrasts, enormous richness and great poverty that live nervously together, creating a tension that can generate futile and destructive energy. The diversity of cultures and communities, the so-called melting pot, confined in narrow spaces, generates an art unique and almost suspect for the rest of the USA for its cosmopolitan, racial and sexual mix and for its liberal profile, at the antipodes of the republican conformism. When the city reached the lowest point of its financial crisis, practically bankrupt, in the mid-1970s, President Gerald Ford refused to issue a federal debt amnesty, also to please the American right wing that hoped to see Big Apple punished for its sins.

Daily News on October 30, 1975.
Ford to City: Drop Dead
WASHINTON, Oct. 29 (News Bureau) - President Ford declared flatly today that he would veto any bill calling for "a federal bail-out of New York City" and instead proposed legislation that would make it easier for the city to go into bankruptcy.[100]

New York's geography is in fact dotted with cultural milestones of all shapes, sizes and importance. Places where art happened and continue to happen. Musicians who come here today can go on pilgrimage to countless places that evoke a historical echo. Be-bop was born from jam

---

[100] http://www.nydailynews.com/new-york/president-ford-announces-won-bailout-nyc-1975-article-1.2405985

sessions at Minton's Playhouse in Harlem, Jimi Hendrix made his American debut at Cafe Wha? in Greenwich Village, while Gerde's Folk City in the West Village was the stage where Bob Dylan held his first concerts in 1961. The Apollo Theatre in Harlem was the testing ground for generations of black musicians, like James Brown and B.B. King. The Disco era took place between the dance floors of Studio 54, Paradise Garage and the Mudd Club. Punk and No Wave settled permanently at GBCB's. There is a synergistic relationship between New York and its music. The city inspires both thanks to the words and the noises produced by its inhabitants. New York works as a refuge for its local artists and for creatives from all over the world attracted by its rich reserve of myths, legends and the cultural energy that seems to run along the walls of its skyscrapers. Attracted by the gentrification of lofts, warehouses and houses located in areas once considered slums, figurative artists, directors, writers, painters and musicians join their forces together by sharing situations and common workplaces[101].

New York. The mecca of all artists, a true gravitational well for anyone wishing to find their way in the alternative artistic community that has long been operating in the Big Apple. Musicians, painters, photographers, intellectuals, writers, journalists, composers. All in search of their inspiration and how to launch their career in Gotham City. Gotham City, a sinister name, a dark knights name that found its base in the profound economic crisis in which the city and its inhabitants had collapsed but which drew its origins in the past of the city itself. Washington Irving was the first to rename New York with this name in 1807, on the pages of Salmagundi magazine. The name is inspired by the English town near Nottingham, whose inhabitants had become famous in English folklore for having foiled all King John's attempts to tax them by pretending to be crazy or stupid. In 1830 James Kirke Paulding inserted "Gotham" in the title of a collection of short stories, "Cronicles of the City of Gotham". Although it should sound ironic or derisory, the term was soon appreciated by the people of New York. Charles Astor Bristed, in his

---

[101] Steve Chick, Psychic Confusion, pag. 11-16.

"The Upper Ten Thousand. Sketches of American Society"(1852) wrote of "our beloved Gotham and in the places to which regular Gothamites - American cockneys, so to speak - are wont to repair"[102]. Then in the 30s and 40s the image of New York began to spread among jazz musicians as a shimmering and promising land, where they could find lavish engagements and the best conditions to promote their music.

Why does New York has this centrality on the geographical and cultural map of the United States? I think there are different reasons: it ranges from its cosmopolitan character, from the dozens of different languages, cultures, traditions and confessions that have made this metropolis since its beginning. The mythopoietic values implicit in its being an island, with all the references that an "island" contains. The dialectic that has always been released between the metropolitan dimension (the port, the fashion industry, the junction of rivers and canals and railways, the network of commerce) and the mosaic of villages around the city. A dialectic that allowed to contain, in the convulsive, turbulent, contradictory way that is proper to New York, different extremes, extremes loved/hated by successive generations of artists fleeing from within (or from outside) the United States.

The economic crisis of the 70s hit New York in an inexorable and brutal way, leaving a disastrous aftermath of abandonment, everywhere in the city. In the 60s, New York's economy had ceased to expand, while municipal spending continued to rise at an annual rate of over 8%. It was a period of big social tensions (the war in Vietnam, crime, violence, drugs, racial tensions), in which politicians desperately tried to respond with expedients to the needs of the community and to the claims of powerful consortiums formed by the municipal employee union organizations. Assistance to the poor and unemployed absorbed an increasing share of resources, while basic services (police, firefighters, public hygiene and education) received less and less more. The repair of school buildings, the textbooks for schools, the maintenance of city streets were neglected.

---

[102] https://archive.org/details/uppertenthousan02brisgoog/page/n295

The budget for public parks was drastically reduced and Senator Daniel Patrick Moynihan argued that the city should hand over its management to the National Park Service, being unable to provide for it anymore. The city was dirty and dangerous.

Let's talk about numbers. In 1975 New York's total revenue was $ 10.9 billion and expenses totaled $ 12.8 billion. The annual budget deficit was close to 2 billion dollars. It depended on stagflation, an economic situation typical of the seventies and inexplicable to most of the classical economic theories. In this case, rising inflation, unemployment without remedies and almost zero growth were joined by an elephantine bureaucracy, ever higher operating costs, and a skyrocketing debt of the Municipality (due to interest on bonds issued). The city repeatedly increased its taxes and became the most expensive place to live in the United States. An unfavorable situation for commercial activities.

In March and April 1975 the 104th mayor of the city, Abe Beame, a politician who certainly was not famous for his cleverness in solving urban problems, found himself on the ropes. In May of that year, New York financially imploded when the institutions that guaranteed the municipal bonds issued by the Municipality to pay their expenses decided to stop the loans to an institution that was considered as high risk. After this brutal exclusion from the credit market (Beame accused the bankers and republican newspapers of "conspiracy"), the city administration lost control of its financial affairs and the state of New York had to give 800 million dollars in advance.

The credit institutions imposed the establishment of the Municipal Assistance Corporation (MAC), commanded by Felix G. Rohatyn, partner of the investment bank Lazard Frères, who exercised considerable influence on the financial fortunes of the metropolis during his mandate (he resigned it in 1993). The MAC issued long-term, high-yield bonds guaranteed by the city's assets to pay creditors, but on one condition: sacrifices, big sacrifices. The City cut services, fired 63,828 municipal employees (including 10,800 teachers and 4,000 hospital employees), in the "first wave of layoffs since the Great Depression" closed fire stations, blocked the free tutoring program for all New York high school graduates attending the city university and the price of the subway access ticket (increasingly degraded by urban "graffiti") skyrocketed from thirty five to fifty cents. As we saw before, October 30, 1975, the attempt to persuade the federal government to smooth out the slopes of the fiscal crisis failed. The Daily News opened with an emblematic title of how the rest of America saw Gotham City: "Ford to City: Drop Dead." Further action was needed and New York went from crisis to crisis for the rest of the decade, while taxes increased further and services deteriorated. The inhabitants of New York, by logical consequence, abandoned the city in increasing numbers. The factories moved to the Sunbelt southern states. The tax base was compromised and municipal debt increased further.

In 1977 the Philadelphia All Stars, a soul and R&B group, launched a phenomenal hit single whose text clearly and concisely denounced the degraded situation in which the American metropolis was: Let's clean up the ghetto.

You know, I was in New York City a few months ago
And the garbage and the Trash men were on strike
I'm talking about the Maintenance people for the city
What they were trying to do was
They were trying to get A little more money
You know, get a little raise in pay
But at that particular time The city was broke
They were about ready to declare default
I tell you, the garbage in some places
Was stacked up two, three stories high...[103]

---

[103] Philadelphia International was founded in Philadelphia in 1971 by Kenny Gamble and Leon Huff. The Philadelphia allstars consisted of Lou Rawls, Billy Paul, Archie Bell, The O'Jays, Teddy Pendergrass & Dee Dee Sharpe Gamble who all got together to make this record with the profits going to a charity programme in 1977, one off Philadelphia labels most socially aware

As the carcass of city's infrastructures decayed, New York artists and musicians began a flourishing of creative activities in order to regain possession of the city. They forged their communities in the void left by deindustrialisation and real estate divestments, outside the commercial channels fueled by industry. Avant-garde artists like Nam June Paik, Joan Jonas and Gordon MattaClark, who created their works in harmony with the new topography of New York, transforming the abandoned Soho warehouses in the most vibrant art community in the world. The "jazz loft" scene was created by free jazz musicians who gathered in abandoned lofts such as Studio We, Studio Rivbea and Ali's Alley, which they had taken over the property, trying to shape an apparently unstructured and penetrating sound, a sound that was called "ecstatic". Young rock musicians, especially those who came from the more peripheral suburbs, found themselves in old theaters such as Mercer Street Art Center or bleak taverns like Max's Kansas City. They reacted to the increasingly pretentious and commercial nature of rock by reducing music at its most basic essence, reaching illumination in the ephemeral waste of trash culture and noise.

Those years found down town involved in a continuous process of social and environmental restructuring. The changes were enormous, including both physical landscapes and their proposed use by industrial, residential and commercial constituencies. Disagreements became rampant between opposing interest groups, causing a series of battles that left the fate of the areas evolving for decades. This instability proved annoying for those with long-term interests in the real estate sector, and it also allowed the rise of unexpected new types of institutions that thrived within this rapidly changing urban wilderness.

Most of the discussions focused on the former factories that dotted the area, whose capacitive and non-partitioned stories were known as lofts. Lofts were built in the late nineteenth century and housed a variety of light industries, including garment manufacturing, printing, machinery manufacturing, textiles, storage and shipping. Their physical

---

songs.

characteristics were designed to facilitate assembly line and the use of small machinery in an era prior to large-scale mass production. The old mezzanine buildings only had free elevators, but the more recent ones also lifts for passengers, the ceilings were twelve to fifteen feet high and often supported by vaulted arches (in smaller buildings) or columns. They showed classic architectural details, reflecting the late 19th century taste for the Italian Renaissance. The columns in the mezzanine buildings were often fluted and the buildings constructed of solid (brick and iron) and valuable materials (oak floors and even copper sills).

Between 1950 and 1970, the percentage of New Yorkers employed in industrial production had fallen from 29.5% to 20.5%, with a loss of over 300,000 jobs. Two main factors had led to this decline: first, more efficient machinery had reduced the need for human labor and, secondly, production had started to migrate out of town to new and larger suburban factories in other parts of the country. Meanwhile the supply of spaces for commercial and industrial use had begun to drastically exceed the demand. Countless public and political debates arose on how to use these areas. Endless debates, which ran from the mid 50s to the early 70s, which made it impossible to know what the next Manhattan's landscape would be, led to prolonged real estate divestment. The owners were reluctant to renovate or even provide maintenance on their buildings, as the outcome of the redevelopment plans could have suddenly made these expenses unnecessary.

Many structures fell into disrepair, attracting abusers and drug addicts and exacerbating the negative perceptions of these areas. Some owners simply abandoned their properties completely, after realizing that they were losing too much money. After the construction of the Cross-Bronx Expressway, even the lower part of Manhattan found itself trapped in a vicious cemetery of financial evisceration, abandonment and urban decay. The middle class escaped, bringing to a wave of abandonment of properties. Building speculators who clung to their buildings, often targeted them with arson, hiring "rent-a-thugs" to burn them to cash in the insurance. Other fires were caused by obsolete electrical systems in

vacant properties, with equally devastating results. In the mid-1970s, 43,000 housing units in the southern Bronx simply vanished. This dismantling was followed by the cancellation of city services, further aggravating the downward spiral of the neighborhoods.
But when these areas became more hostile to residents and expensive for owners, they slowly began to attract a somewhat unexpected new population of residents: artists. Painters and visual artists were the first to crowd into lofts, where open floors and abundant quantities of natural material favored the creation of large-scale works. In addition to using them as private homes and workplaces, some artists also opened their lofts for exhibitions and sales as public galleries. Above all, the excess of available space pushed the owners to rent them at remarkably low price. The residence was technically illegal due to current zoning restrictions, but for many artists the possibility of a large, low-priced space offset the risk of possible evictions[104]. Saxophone player Mark Whitecage thus recalls his own arrival in 1967 in the nice book made by Michael C Heller, "Loft Jazz Improvising". Whitecage gravitated to the Lower East Side, an area just east of SoHo that became known for low rents and a high concentration of musicians.

"I found a pad for fifty-seven dollars a month. I could work a couple days a month to pay for that. So money was easy in those days because the rents were so low ... The whole town was full of musicians. Youd walk down the street in the spring and the windows would open up. You'd hear a trombone player up there, a violin over here. All these guys have been shedding all winter and they finally open the windows! You'd hear them all."[105]

John Zorn also recalls in an interview with William Duckworth the low cost of rents:

---

[104] MichaelC. Heller, Loft Jazz Improvising New York in the 1970s, pag 26-28.
[105] MichaelC. Heller, Loft Jazz Improvising New York in the 1970s, pag 33.

DUCKWORTH: Were you making any money by this point?
ZORN: No, nothing. Nothing at all. My apartment was $50 a month. It went up to $75 in 1978 and I couldn't afford to live there anymore, so I moved here. And I paid $50 a month here until about 1986.[106]

These memories are further confirmed by Zorn in the booklet accompanying the cd/dvd of "James Moore plays The Book of Heads":

"By 1976 I could negotiate guitar, bass, piano, organ, sax, Hute, clariner, trombone, tuba and classical percussion to varying degrees, but my main focus of activiry continued to be composition,
I had written 2 operas, dozens of solo, chamber and symphonic works, a handful of early game pieces that explored a varying synthesis of improvisation and composition, some graphic scores, tape pieces and even some minima! Experiments. I was practicing the saxophone 10 hours a day and was improvising in a very noise oriented and idiosyncratic style living and working in the East Village was like being in a creative crucible - music was everywhere and finding like minded musicians was nor difficult. We played on the street to help make ends meet and did spontaneous concerts in parks We met often and talked at concerts, movie theaters, jam sessions, book and record stores. In the summertime one could hear musicians practicing out of their windows and sometimes we would yell up at them or even find our way to their door to talk music or jam More and more musicians were being drawn to this bombed out area of New York where you could easily find an apartment for $50 a month, and where you could hear some of the most amazing live music on the planet. Studio Rivbea, The Five Spot, LaMama, etc., CBGB and Someplace Nice were all thriving and we went regularly (usually listening from out on the street). Phillip Johnston, Polly Bradfield, Wayne Horvitz, Louie Belogenis and Mark E Miller were just a few of che early regulars on the scene, and by 1978-9 Fred Frith, Ned Rochenberg, Anthony Coleman, Ikue Mori, George Lewis, Bill Laswell,

---

[106] Duckworth, Talking Music,pag. 459.

Kramer, Bob Ostertag, Robert Dick, Tom Cora, Toshinori Kondo and many others were also living in close proximity."

But it wasn't over yet. In his book ""In The Seventies: Adventures in the Counter-Culture"" Barry Miles writes that on July 13, 1977 he was at the Boz Scaggs's concert in the Alice Tully Hall at the Lincon Center in New York, together with his friend and photographer Joe Steven. Halfway through the show, at nine-twenty-seven PM, the power went out. First they thought it was a momentary breakdown, then they realized that the whole city was turned off. The audience broke into a roar, as if it was a great rock moment. It was chaos, more than 4,000 people remained closed in the subway, the traffic lights were down, the police was present at some road crossing, others had been invaded by crazy people who were waving, blowing in their whistles and causing accidents. Down in Brooklyn, two blocks from Broadway, which divides Bushwich from Bedford-Stuyvesantt, they were buildings on fire, 194 stores had been looted and 45 burned. The police made the biggest arrest in the New York's history, that throw into prison 3,776 jackals, not to mention those who got away with it. A total of 1600 shops were raided and over a thousand fires started. A congress study calculated that the damage amounted to more than $ 300 million. On that night, during the blackout, the New Yorkers who looked up showed the stars: the last time it had happened was during the blackout in 1965[107].

---

[107] Barry Miles, I Settanta pag. 234 -236.

Doctor Eugene Chadbourne

Let's go back to our first-person detective novel for a moment. Our narrator, the creative mind behind this complicated Victorian mechanism, is a composer who has decided to write a series of guitar studies based on a complex mix of composition, graphic writing and improvisation. This series is an open work, open to the decisions made by those who decide to play these studies, but at the same time immersed in a particular cultural, musical, social and economic humus. A humus, a gomi, which Zorn has been able to adequately use and in turn fertilize with his ideas and creations. But to create a detective story, the voice of a narrator is not enough, we also need an investigator, an interpreter, someone who knows how to decipher its plot for us. For the listeners.
Already in college Zorn sensed how important it was to compose but also to play and attract around himself a group of musicians able to share, understand and execute his ideas. At those times improvisation and composition returned to come together in a creative and functional way. Philip Glass was working with his ensemble; Steve Reich had created his own. Their example, the fact that they had created their own ensemble and that they performed their own music in the company of other musicians, had a great influence on Zorn, even more than their academic career.[108] Harry Partch had been another who had created his own groups and worked closely with the musicians to create different music. There was already something similar in jazz, blues or rock traditions. Maybe there was also in the classical world many years before, but all this had disappeared, replaced by the most popular romantic image of the composer enclosed in a kind of ivory tower. Zorn reiterated the importance of having close relationships with musicians, tired of the kind of overly intellectual and very unemotional approach towards which a lot of contemporary classical music moved. He wanted something different, something that affected the stomach and emotions but at the same time

---
[108] Bill Milkowski, Rockers, Jazzbos & Visionaries, pag. 225.

had the structural complexity that contemporary classical music had already achieved[109].

The first ones to join Zorn were the violinist Polly Bradfield and the guitarist Eugene Chadbourne. After separating from Joe Foster and Philip Johnny, who worked in a band called Microscopic Septet, closer to the jazz tradition, our composer met Chadbourne and Bradfield, Fred Frith, Tom Cora and Wayne Horvitz. One by one, people gravitated towards New York and somehow got involved in the creative vortex of the new generation of improvisers[110]. A network of relationships was created, with small clubs to play in and a loyal audience.

"In meeting Eugene Chadbourne in 1976 I found a kind of soulmate and we began to work together and hang on a daily basis, talking about a huge variety of music, films, books, philosophy and more. He was one of my first serious musical colleagues and we shared a lot of the same passions, imagining ourselves as a kind of "Bird and Diz." We toured together, released self-produced records, made posters, played on each others' compositions and improvised with a wide range of musicians and non-musicians, performing coundess gigs in and around New York, often at my apartment across from the Public Theater - a six floor walkup to an artist studio at 430 Lafayerre Street that was the first home of the Theatre of Musical Optics."[111]

BOH were written, between 1976 and 1978, specifically for Eugene

---

[109] "I was tired of the kind of overly intellectual, very dry approach that a lot of contemporary classical music was moving towards. I wanted like a real kick-butt kind of thing. There was an emotional aspect to the new romanticism, but even that seemed very sterile to me. I wanted someone who was up there, you know, blowing his guts out, but I also wanted the structural complexity that contemporary classical music had reached." William Duckworth, Talking Music pag. 452.

[110] Bill Milkowski, Rockers, Jazzbos & Visionaries, pag. 230.

[111] Notes from the cd "James Moore Plays The Book Of Heads - CD and DVD of a film by Stephen Taylor", Tzadik, 2015.

Chadbourne, and basically incorporated all the strangest sounds that could be created on the instrument at the time, using specific Chadbourne's techniques of playing in the second half of the 70s (toy balloons, a bow, a slide, clothespins, pencils, mbira keys, talking dolls, whisks...) and other ideas developed by a group of skilled and unscrupulous improvisers: Frith, Sharrock, Bailey, Kaiser, Duck Bake, Davey Williams, etc.

Eugene Chadbourne is not an easy artist to describe. Born in 1954 and raised in Boulder, Colorado, he started playing the guitar after seeing the Beatles on television at the Ed Sullivan TV Show. His unique and personal style seems to be the bizarre result of a complex genetic cross between folk protest and free improvisation, noisecore and virtuosity, Country & Western and free Jazz. A form so deliberately contradictory, so ridiculously incompatible, that it simply seems perverse. His prolific record production is characterized by freeform guitar, salacious beats, satire, political comments, frightening noises and bizarre chaos, a double assault on both classic formalism and rock romanticism. Healthy carrier of a defined aesthetic, he has no scruple about manifesting his blatant hostility towards the gleaming patina of high culture. The cracked details of his artistic form define it as a product of the 60s counterculture, Captain Beefheart, marijuana, Phil Ochs, the anti-Vietnam war protests, John Coltrane....

"I've always been a big fan of solos. I love bearing groups where somebody 'takes a solo', it's very very nice. One thing that might be lacking in improvised musc where everyone's always active is that you don't have soloists."[112]

Between 1976 and 1977, practically in the same time span in which the BOH were composed, Chadbourne released on the Parachute label three solo albums of pure guitar improvisation, where we can find many ideas

---

[112] Ben Watson, "Hobo trails and boho trials", The Wire, Issue 177, November 1998, pag.50.

which were then taken up in Zorn's compositions[113]. The close relationship between Zorn and Chadbourne then hovers over the whole cd box of game pieces "John Zorn - The Parachute Years 1977 - 1980 (Lacrosse Hockey Pool Archery)"[114], where the guitarist performs "Lacrosse", "Hockey" and "Archery" in various versions. Basically at the time he and Zorn joined together punk music, the idea of an open work and radical improvisation in sound challenges for all the three types of audience, when they had an audience available. Chadbourne's assault on the impersonality of the record product extends not only to the public, but also to the media he uses for publications. In an era where everyone speaks digital and the internet, his preferences still go towards analogue cassettes, more or less unconsciously imitating the "samizdat"[115] culture of pre-89 Eastern Europe and of today's Africa.

Chadbourne's prodigious production could match that of his longtime colleague Zorn, but the strategically overlooked spread of his works could not be drastically different from the refined editions of Avant/Tzadik, through which Zorn channels his music. If Zorn tries to gain complete control over everything he has ever done and everything he will ever do[116], the guitarist prefers to focus on distributive chaos, aiming more at the indiscriminate diffusion of his messages. A provocation that talks about a confused sense of a reappropriation of the imaginary, which again is citation, recovery, unearthing of the removed and fascination for primitive, archaic forms, outdated by the times, remixed in a low fi form and that exude an intense and captivating energy.

To appreciate and understand his unusual guitar technique (Leon McAuliffe meets Fred 'Sonic' Smith meets Derek Balley), the way to play

---

[113] Volume One: Solo Acoustic Guitar (Parachute, 1976)
Volume Two: Solo Acoustic Guitar (Parachute, 1976)
Volume Three: Guitar Trios (Parachute, 1977)
[114] https://www.discogs.com/it/John-Zorn-The-Parachute-Years-1977-1980-Lacrosse-Hockey-Pool-Archery/release/354549
[115] https://en.wikipedia.org/wiki/Samizdat
[116] Frank Zappa had a very similar entrepreneurial attitude.

his banjo (the traditional bluegrass meets the clawhammer), and his musical ability, often wrapped in an aura of boring anti-experimental holiness, it is better to listen to him playing alive and through his record production. Chadbourne has managed to transform his own modus operandi into a distinctive style. His method is to bring out his extraordinary productions in the world, always remaining true to himself. The flood of publications on small labels, his own "guerrila cassettes", his openness to collaboration and pure accident suggest that maximizing profits is not the only viable strategy and that his avant-garde hoboism and DIY ethics are the proof that the economic emancipation of the musician will always have to be implemented by the musicians themselves.

Musical theater: Theatre of Musical Optics

In 1974/75 Zorn founded the Theater of Musical Optics, a laboratory in which to perform live some of the pieces present in his youthful anthology "First Recordings" (1995) in concerts / performances that were held in the laboratory itself, often located in the only place available: the loft where Zorn lived. In addition to Zorn, many musicians acted in the Theater. Basically, two different types of concerts took place. In the first Zorn played a musical instrument: as a saxophonist and composer, he appeared regularly with a group of musicians, dedicating himself to "improvised music" or "music for improvisers", who acted on the basis of precise indications, manipulating carefully selected, orchestrated objects. In the second type of concert he performed alone in collected situations, using small objects in visual function, as if they were musical "notes". These "object shows" were staged at the Anthology Film Archives, at the Collective for the Living Cinema and at the Ontological-Hysteric Theater but most of the time they were staged in his small studios on Lafayeue Street and the Lower East Side, where the necessary concentration was obtained by keeping the audience below twelve spectators, with an average of five and minimum, not too unusual, peaks of two. The audience was made up mostly by friends and acquaintances. Sometimes posters were posted, but they rarely had an address on: just a phone number, to call for booking. Usually the posters or notices were spread by Zorn himself, sometimes the posters were posted after the end of a show.

During the evolution of these shows Zorn realized that visual manipulation represented the musical fulcrum of these compositions. This pushed him to progressively eliminate the sounds until he reached the central nucleus: the object itself, in a sequence that is legible following the evolution described by works such as "Fidel" (1979) where both the sound and the time of execution were successively eliminated . What was left? The essence of music, or the objects of music: anything can become a musical instrument and, consequently, any noise can become, or rather, be music if properly placed in an organized context. Also in 1974 Zorn discovered Richard Foreman's theater. The Ontological-Hysteric Theater was founded in New York by the playwright, dramatist and director Richard Foreman in 1968, with the aim of making the intangible visible, bringing the static tensions that unite and divide individuals into the spotlight, publicly unveiling the mechanisms that regulate interpersonal relationships. Technically it was a 'total theater' that combined drama, philosophy, psychoanalysis, literature, visual arts and performance. Fidel was an example of this visual theater, an example very similar to the BOH aesthetic. In Fidel the objects were presented one after the other. On a black table and inside a white frame, the object was read by its position, its shadows, the action and the duration: all variables that changed imperceptibly but constantly. Fidel was a condensed equation, consisting of units repeated several times.

The same base was always used: a white square on a black cloth, a sort of inverted score. The same action was constantly repeated, placing an object or a set of objects always with the same purpose. Although the apparatus of lattices, lights and objects was reduced to a minimum, it derived from the selection among a wide variety of elements used in the previous shows, with the purpose to alter the context in which an object was presented. For Zorn, music could exist on a purely visual level or it could use other means, other than sound. In his first pieces the first musical elements on which he decided to intervene were rhythm and melody, taking care of them in a very simple way, using them like objects.

Following Cage's lesson, where by subtracting every element from music, what remained, the most important element and which characterizes it as music, was time, Zorn created compositional grids that corresponded to a kind of object music, where the grid was the score. "Fidel", like BOH, showed that every used object had its own time in itself: if an object or a familiar sound, which can be recognized, say for 5 seconds, is presented to us and subsequently we are exposed to an object or sound that we don't know, during its 5 seconds the mind continues to think, to try to identify it, to contemplate different possibilities. As a result those 5 seconds may seem different in duration and intensity from the 5 seconds spent looking at something familiar. Perception makes the difference. "Fidel", like BOH, turns a concert into a semiotic show. A concert performance, whether you want it or not, is also a potential theater.

Everything happens in a homogeneous and unanimous time. In a musical theater as in BOH the relationship between the time of music and the time of the scene, between what you listen to and what you see, can differentiate itself, can become estranged and can become very complex. Observing a scenic apparatus, even the most minimal and scarce, implies a subjectively variable and discontinuous temporal dimension. It is a bit like looking at a picture, a landscape or reading a book: we can go back, we can close our eyes, we can focus on a detail. For those who listen to music time is obviously irreversible, it is like lived time that accumulates different qualities of time and which can only be accessed with memory. But in musical theater, listening is certainly the strongest and most resistant dimension.

In the dialogue between the two temporalities, music and image, it's the quality of time of music that takes over and that allows us to analyze and comment on what lies before our eyes, conditioning their perception. BOH are close to an idea of musical theater which is a theater of the mind and memory, perhaps a virtual theater, where our attention oscillates between visions and listening, in the continuous search for different perspectives. Zorn, with BOH, has created a theater that is not necessarily made intelligible only by the specific things we see or by the objects that interact with the interpreter's guitar but also by the desire to penetrate, discover and confuse the different times of the music and of what we see. Sounds don't age like ideas. I don't think that, in music, the important thing is to generate new sounds and unprecedented sound situations but rather to generate conceptual organisms capable of generating new narratives.

Traditional score against graphic notation

It all began around 840 AD., when a monk named Aureliano di Réôme created one of the first examples of western musical notation. It was a basic attempt to create a musical theory treatise called Disciplina musica. From the Baroque era in Europe, composers wanted to exhibit their work more consistently and to leave interpretation less open to the artists. They sought and created a refined and codified musical language. A language that composers like Beethoven, then Gustav Mahler at the end of the 19th century, endeavored to free from traditional boundaries. Their orchestral scores are full of scribbles, footnotes and signs, as if sticking to the rules was too much or too little for them. The real turning point came at the beginning of the 20th century, composers like Henry Cowell (Menlo Park, 11 March 1897 - New York, 10 December 1965) began experimenting with notation and its new musical resources were a radical attempt to change the way to write music. During the twentieth century and after the horrors of the Second World War, there was a growing feeling among composers that traditional Western notation was inadequate to express their musical ideas. Composers have always struggled to express themselves and in the Twentieth Century, many began using this radical graphic approach to their music. The first example of a complete graphic score was Morton Feldman's "Projection 1" (1950) for solo cello. It features a completely original notation, which looks more like a circuit diagram. It looks forward to its times. During the 50s and 1960s, a new generation of radical post-war composers such as Krzysztof Penderecki, Karlheinz Stockhausen, John Cage, Roman Haubenstock-Ramati began using graphic notation as a serious and necessary alternative to traditional forms of notation.

Probably the pinnacle of graphic notation belongs to a piece by Cornelius Cardew, entitled "Treatise" (1963-1967). The piece consists of 193 pages of highly abstract sheet music. This is the Sistine Chapel of notation. His training as a graphic designer is obvious. He also used the principles of cognitive psychology, which is central to design. Cardew's motivation was to inspire the performer's creativity and interpretation. The score did not provide specific instructions on how to play the piece, not even which instruments to use. It's a dense piece, which allows multiple explorations and interpretations and it can prove to be a rewarding experience. With the increasing complexity and abstraction of music, the different types of composition increased, some bordering on incomprehensibility, but with a real graphic beauty.

Brian Eno is one of the best known contemporary musicians who use graphic notation. Eno is very explicit about not having received formal musical education and therefore not being able to annotate in an orthodox way. He used graphic scores out of necessity and made it an integral part of his creative process. Anyone who is processing a notation will try to minimize the probability of errors. But this is a technical problem, completely unrelated to the requirement of disjunction. What distinguishes a real notation is not the ease or otherwise of making correct judgments, but the consequences that derive from it.

A score is a character of a notional system. Standard musical notation offers a familiar and meaningful whole, at the same time it's complex, practical and common to users of different verbal languages. No alternative has gained any diffusion and no other culture has developed over the centuries any effective musical notation comparable to this. The monopoly held for a long time by the standard musical notation has sparked a multiplicity of rebellions and alternative proposals that testify to the authority it has reached. Composers complain from time to time that scores written according to this notation prescribe too many or too few aspects or the wrong aspects, or they prescribe the right ones but in a way that is too much or not sufficiently precise. In a broader sense, this revolution may propose a greater or a lesser or a different control over the means of production.

Design and music intersect in many ways; fashion, album covers, set design and intruments. Graphic notation is no exception, although it is a relatively unknown side outside the sometimes rarefied world of orchestral and experimental music. Graphic notation works the same way as traditional musical notation, but uses abstract symbols, images and text to convey meaning to the performers. The visual comparison between traditional and modern graphic notation can be surprising. Traditional notation is linear and rigid, but of rapid and effective consultation for those who have received formal education. Modern graphic notation is open, it can offer flexibility and allow the performer to interpret the composer's ideas, but at the same time it can generate confusion and uncertainty.

The score

"Toy ballons, talking dolls, mbira keys, wet fingers whops, whisks, knocks, multiple harmonics: these 35 études for solo guitar, composed in 1978 for Eugene Chadbourne, give a new meaning to the word 'virtuoso'."[117]

BOH represent an interesting example of how a series of graphic scores designed for musical studies can become something much more semiotic, in which the sign is transposed from one purpose to another. In a sense, BOH say that music should no longer be self-referential. No more self-referential thinking about contemporary music, with the abandonment of a dominant position by the composer, in a similar but reversed way with respect to Cage's ideas. No more self-referential in the sense of the improviser, who agrees to operate on structures defined by others who can leave their stylistic path and their imaginary, No more self-referential in the sense of the figure of music itself, who can look at other ideas and other aspects of our society. All this without taking itself too seriously.

In the first part of the book we saw how, from certain points of view, Zorn is a curious and complicated mix, a sort of hybridization between a classical composer, a jazz musician, a radical improviser, a musical entrepreneur, a pop music expert, a record collector, a passionate cinephile and a careful analyzer of the cultural and urban community that surrounds him. His absolute dedication to art, an almost nerdy and pure workaholic dedication, led him to understand how the new developments of contemporary music can be happily translated through popular music in the way in which composition and improvisation can unite themselves thanks to musicians with an extraordinary level of openness. With BOH Zorn leaves the scores of his more classically academic compositions, leaves the role of conductor in his game pieces, leaves his role of radical improviser to create hybrids that give a new meaning to all the musical

---

[117] Notes from the obi of the cd "John Zorn The Book of Heads", Tzadik, 1995.

structures that surround him in the New York's cultural sphere.
In a sense, these scores certify the role of Zorn as a "cultural reporter" in representing, distilling the New York 1976 - 1978 alternative cultural and musical scene into a sort of thirty-five small musical haikus for guitar. He carefully followed what happened in the underground of those years, he understood the best that was achieved in terms of musical creativity and social behavior and condensed it into thirty-five graphic scores, creating at the same time a tradition that could continue to evolve in the years to come through new generations of guitarists.
From a musical point of view, BOH are the equivalent of Tom Johnson's book "The Voice of New Music"[118], a distillate with a high semiotic, cultural, visual, expressive density of what happened in those years when New York fought an artistic struggle against a deep moral, economic, architectural and environmental degradation.
If we analyze the BOH's scores in a purely functional way, we certainly do not find great differences between the layout of a medical examination: the differences arise from the fact that we refer to two different systems of interpretation and reading. The Books of Heads belong to an iconographic system light years away from the romantic rhetorical vision according to which the text says, wants and does thanks to the emanation of some sort of thaumaturgical communicative virtue. In the BOH the symbols do not decide which system they belong to, but we, ourselves, decide by assigning them to that or this system what symbols it is. The motivations that push us to decide in this or the other sense may also depend not on the object itself but on what we know about its history, its institutional function, the behavioral practices in which it is presented to us. A sum of instructions which, far from being contained in it, establishes what it will contain. This does not mean that the assumption or not of an aesthetic fact is a subjective and arbitrary fact. The object must reveal itself jointly with our expectations by exhibiting

---

[118] Tom Johnson, The Voice of New Music: New York City, 1972-1982 - A Collection of Articles Originally Published in the Village Voice, Het Apollohuis, 1989. http://tvonm.editions75.com/

appropriate symbolic traits. Our decisions must be guided by factual knowledge, institutionalized prescriptions and social practices that articulate and make possible any symbolic activity. The aesthetic attitude is a mobile attitude, a search for exploration, this is a model of reception, an aesthetic complement to a more general vision of knowledge. In this sense, BOH are an open and opaque work, opaque because certain methods of reference are in place. BOH are configurable as a classification model for improvisation, the way the figures and descriptions are so classified in the studies are far from rigid or stable and do not lend themselves to univocal codification. Boundaries change and merge, new categories are emerging and the canons of classification are less clear than practice itself.

Value judgments only touch each other incidentally. Critical canons are not offered, no binding judgment is implied, the reader is invited to replace them with the examples he prefers. The word symbol is used as a general and neutral term, which includes letters, texts, words, notes, signs, models and so on, but without hidden references. The goal is to keep as much as possible what originality exemplifies, in addition to what it says. Even a gesture can denote or exemplify. But why do these hints, these negligible movements become so significant when they are related to criticism? Their significance is simply that of labels amplified in the analysis, organization and recording of what we listen to. Musical expression is no less relative and changeable than facial and gestural expression. The boundaries of expression, determined by the difference between exemplification and process and by the differences between metaphysical and literal, are inevitably blurred and transitory.

BOH present a sort of free cadence where at the performer is left a wide margin of initiative and where the scores present congruence classes that properly include those of other scores with their passages sometimes specified note by note. In BOH it is difficult to assess whether an execution is strictly congruent to one sign rather than another. I am not commenting on the question of whether adopting a system like the BOH system would be a good idea. I do not have the competence and it is not my job to make such a judgment. I simply limit myself to pointing out that here is implicit something more than just a passage from one notational system to another. There are only executions subsequent to that single corpus of studies, just as there are drawings and paintings subsequent to a sketch, a bit like in medieval musical manuscripts and in Renaissance lute tablatures: sometimes avant-garde means temporal regression.

Certainly with the BOH it is not possible to create purely autobiographical works. BOH place themselves in a microcosm between the impressive notation, where the relationships between the notes, the approximate limits of their areas and the musical graphs are indicated to the maximum. Different executions of a meticulous score are by no means exact duplicates of each other but can vary widely and in many ways. When a musical language shows a few first characters and few congruence principles simple enough so as to make it easy and almost automatic to use, we tend to consider this language as a tool. When there are many first characters and complex congruence principles so that often the interpretation of a character requires decisions, we tend to say that we must understand language. By making a comparison with architecture, scores, like architectural plans, can sometimes define works in broader terms than we commonly understand them. The performance of a work not only belongs to or is congruent with the work and the score, but also exemplifies it. And since the works and the scores belong to a notational system, we have an exemplification of something that is articulated, disjointed and limited. Furthermore, for musical performance, the exemplification and the expression go far beyond the opera or the score.

"When John Zorn first asked me to play and record the Book of Heads, I felt the way a guitarist feels when an important composer asks them to premiere their work: honored. I then took the scores home and stared at them for a long time in complete bewilderment. Virtually every note involved some sort of extended technique, non-traditional notation or

nearly impossible juxtaposition.
This was not surprising, given the task that Zorn had set for himself: to compose in the language of the late 70's/early 80's "free improv" guitarists (Eugene Chadbourne, Fred Frith, Derek Bailey), a language that most had assumed to be unnotable.
Nor was my bewilderment surprising. My relation to "free improv" guitar playing at the time it was being developed was mostly as a listener. It is one thing to be amazed by the records and performances that were coming out of this scene. It is quite another to make musical sense out of whoops, scrapes, and squeaks, using balloons, nail files. pipe cleaners and alligator clips. Anyone can make a sound. But to "speak", to make music. you have to first own the language. And this takes not only time. but faith thar the language is worth owning, worth knowing.
I believe that the language of the free improv players is not only worth knowing, but maybe even essential to know for contemporary guitarists, not only because the process imposed by these unfamilier techniques is a healthy Zen slap in the face far those too mesmerized (or bored by) their own chops, or because it is nice to have a few extra weird guitar sounds available; it is worth it because, as anyone who has witnessed a free improv performance knows *something amazing happens*, and it's important to try to figure out what that *something* is, what makes it happen and how it can be composed with.
Zom composes in this language with an incredible attention to detail and nuance, and an equally incredible inside knowledge of the guitar, its possibilities and impossibilities. Whether I succeded in bringing any of this out in the performance is not for me to say, but the process of making this record changed the way I hear the guitar. That doesn't happen every day."[119]

This characteristic is the result of the congruence between the written text and additional, verbal or not, instructions, printed together with the score

---

[119] Marc Ribot from the notes on the booklet of the cd "John Zorn The Book of Heads", Tzadik, 1995.

or tacitly transmitted, orally or implicitly, by tradition. These instructions cannot be considered as integral parts of the score, because they belong to a not limited syntactically and semantically dense system, not to a notational language. The exemplification of all that is not prescribed by the score is like the pictorial exemplification, a matter of different measurements and calculations. Thanks to its connotation code, reading a score is always a historical question: it depends on the knowledge of the reader just as if it was a language, intelligible only to those who have learned the signs. In various respects the ideographic language of the Book of Heads recalls certain languages in which analog and signal units are mixed together, with the difference however that the ideogram is experienced as a sign, while the score is seen as a representation of reality, a series of instructions for performing a creative process. In his way John Zorn is a rhetorician, his score is a laboratory of tropes.

BOH are like an archive open to reinvention and this musical archeology can reveal art trends and show their future potential. BOH are topophilic places that can keep us in their psycho-geographic-musical design and guide our stories. They are conceptually dense, they are like a space that includes images of built or undeveloped places that are part of a varied collective practice marked by a multiplicity of stories, social perspectives and intersubjective fantasies. BOH are a composed mental image: a stratified form of representation of a musical culture that tries to bring together two opposing cultural poles: composition and improvisation.

Giuliana Bruno in her essay "Surface: Matters of Aesthetics, Materiality, and Media"[120] rightly observes how modern aesthetics rest on the idea that places, as well as artistic objects, can't be separated from the observer: the aesthetic experience is haptic when it tangibly establishes a close transient relationship between art and the observer, in this case between the music and the listener. Zorn conceives this empathy with the

---

[120] Giuliana Bruno, Surface: Matters of Aesthetics, Materiality, and Media, University of Chicago Press, 2014.

listener as a series of projections towards the whole and the outside, between what moves in an artistic object and what moves the listener and that moves within him. All these textural aspects contribute to create the atmosphere of these scores. Zorn challenges the flatness of the score moving towards a cultural three-dimensionality. On the surface of the BOH there is a mnemonic mood, these designs may appear two-dimensional, but they function as if they were environmental sculptures that come to life in a mobile interpretive reception. In Zorn's musical world you can come across an archeology of different materials, objects, characters and landscapes. In BOH's scores every object, every gesture, even the freest, the most mobile seems to be framed. The "miniaturization" doesn't depend from the dimension, from the time spent in the execution, but from a sort of precision that the representation of the score puts in delimiting, in ending. This precision is nothing reasonable or moral: the boundaries in the BOH are not clear in a puritanical way but rather thanks to a fracture that takes away the meaning and subtracts any uncertainty. This frame is invisible, it is not surrounded, illuminated, it is not limited by a clear outline, around it there is emptiness, a space that makes it opaque. The corridors, the paths of the BOH are traced according to an idea of rarefaction, like Chinese boxes, one contained within the other up to the void, a sort of semantic meditation. Geometric, rigorously designed, yet somewhere always marked by a fold, by a knot, by an asymmetry, with a care and a technique that recalls the Japanese culture, the scores of the BOH become objects themselves. These graphic scores are tangible thought.

The Book of Heads and the open work

In BOH the interpreter, the performer is no longer a means, an intermediary, but a close collaborator, an investigator. He receives a more or less precise action plan, a certain number of structures which he can combine in the way that is most congenial to him. Again the composition is no longer something already done, but rather something to be done, something made to be adapted. From a means of communication it becomes a means of cooperation and this kind of open form has sometimes necessitated new conceptions of the notation itself based quantitatively and qualitatively not only on the notes but also on the actions. All this is directly connected to the poetics of the open work.[121]

In the BOH we are immediately struck by a macroscopic difference between this kind of musical communication and those to which the classical tradition had accustomed us. In elementary terms, this difference can be formulated in this way: a classical musical work, Aida or Beethoven's symphonies, consisted of a set of sound realities that the author organized in a defined and closed way, offering it to the listener through a structure of conventional signs designed to guide the performer, so that it could substantially produce the form imagined by the composer.

The BOHs instead consist not in a uniquely organized form, but in a possibility of various organizations entrusted to the interpreter's initiative and therefore present themselves not as finished works that ask to be revisited and understood in a given structural direction, but as open works, which are carried out by the interpreter at the same time in which it enjoys them aesthetically.

Each fruition of BOH is thus an interpretation and a performance, because each time the work lives again in an original perspective.

This poetics tends to promote conscious acts of freedom in the interpreter, placing him as the active center of a network of inexhaustible

---

[121] Umberto Eco, Opera aperta. Forma e indeterminazione nelle poetiche contemporanee, Bompiani, 2013.

relationships between which he establishes his own form, without being determined by a need that prescribes him the definitive ways of organizing the work itself. Zorn offers the interpreter a work to be completed, he doesn't know exactly how the BOH can be completed, but he always knows that it will be his work, not another and that at the end of the interpretative dialogue a Form will have materialized, although specifically defined in a way that he could not completely predict in 1976-1978. The BOH performed by two different guitarists will never appear the same, but will never be something absolutely pointless. They will never be the same version even if performed in two different moments by the same guitarist. Intended, they will be as factual realizations of a highly individualized format whose assumptions are found in the graphics and instructions offered by Zorn himself.

The composer provides the interpreter with starting points, general lines of action, proposals and suggestions to which the performer must always respond in a new way. Howerve, for this to happen, everything must be carefully planned in terms of musical organization. I could say that the greater the freedom granted to the interpreter and the public, the more complex the structure of the composition becomes and consequently the more difficult the composer's work becomes. He must prevent chaos from destroying all possible relationships. When the tendency to give freedom to the interpreter is brought to its extreme limits, the composer is condemned to give up making free decisions, to no longer give any sign for any interpretation. Consequently, the results will not stabilise, the message opens to an infinite number of different outcomes, the information increases considerably. Taking this imprecision and this information to the extreme limit, exasperating the co-presence of all the sounds, thickening the plot, what we will have is White Noise, the undifferentiated sum of all the frequencies, where the information becomes a confused opaque canvas. In BOH, the emphasis is on the process, on the possibility of identifying many possibilities, in the knowledge of the basic language. Eco writes that the reception of a message structured in an open way means that the expectation of what we are talking about does not imply a forecast of the expected as much as a wait for the unexpected[122]. BOH are a vocabulary, a cipher, born in a particular historical moment. The study of a case.

---

[122] Umberto Eco, Opera Aperta pag 147.

Urban and musical congestion

In BOH, time is under pressure, demonstrating resistance to the growing technological privatization of time and space of resources going on today. We have seen how Zorn derives many elements of BOH from the musical iconography set by the New York music scene of the 70s and by his musicians friends in the Parachute Years but also how he composes them in a single programmatic structure in which the presence of each element is indispensable for increase the impact on others. Creation and destruction are the poles that define the field of Manhattan's scratchy culture, Zorn with his BOH creates a magic carpet that is able to reproduce experiences and recreate almost any kind of sensation; support an almost unlimited number of ritual representations and interpretations which exorcise the risks of temporal stylistic decay; survive the onslaught of time and musical mutations.

The proposed issues, tactics and solutions anticipate in an almost exemplified way and summarize the tortuous misunderstandings between official culture and popular culture, between elitist taste and popular imagination, which torment and will torment the century we are still living for a long time. If we contrast BOH to Manhattan, they almost represent an architectural grid in which all the musical blocks, the studies that compose them, are stylistically identical and equivalent according to the undeclared philosophical of the Manhattan Architectural Grid itself. The transformation, the different interpretation of only one of these aspects affects all the others as a latent possibility: theoretically every studio can turn into a self-sufficient musical enclave, in a dried up archipelago of sounds. In certain semiological aspects, the BOH represent a radical simplification of the concept of improvisation and composition, a formula that allows infinite growth and regeneration without corresponding loss of legibility, legitimacy, intimacy and coherence.

In each representation, a musical building is freed from the excess of shallow effects. The musical architecture of the BOH all together form a matrix of terribly serious frivolities, a vocabulary of poetic formulas that supplants traditional objective planning in favor of a new type of metaphorical planning related to a situation created by a music scene founded on the non-quantifiable. The musical congestion of styles and genres is the essential condition for realizing each of these metaphysics which are these 35 studies. Only co-management is able to generate this mutant musical architecture. Each study represents a different lifestyle and ideology. In each study, the culture of congestion arranges new and stimulating human-musical activities in unprecedented combinations. Thanks to their structure and the freedoms of improvisation it becomes possible for the interpreter to reproduce all situations from the most natural to artificial as and when desired.

If the culture of congestion is the culture of the Twentieth Century[123], the modern spirit that animates the BOH is not a new recipe for creating new music and scores, but the search for something more characteristic and vital as an expression of contemporary activity and thought .

The culture of interpretation has now triggered a paradoxical tradition of the latest fashion and in order to preserve itself it is forced to juggle incessantly between self-destruction and philological thought, trying to continually get rid of its previous incarnation. Every musical container that establishes these tendencies in a certain place, sooner or later degenerates into an accumulation of conditionings, recordings, transcriptions and revisions that prevent that rapid change that the raison d'etre of tradition. Listening to the various versions and interpretations of the BOH recalls the architectural cannibalism at the basis of the Manhattan urban model: incorporating its predecessors, the latest version collects all the energy and spirit of the previous ones and preserves their memory.

BOH is not simply the end product of a long family tree, but rather it represents the summa, the simultaneous existence, in a single place, at a precise moment, of all its lost phases. The score is used as a constructivist social condenser: a machine for generating and intensifying desirable

---

[123] Rem Kolhass, Delirius New York, The Monacelli Press, New York, 1994.

forms of human interactions. Zorn's compositional and organizational talent manages to suspend the irreconcilable differences between mutually intransigent positions in terms of style and logic, composition and improvisation. In a sense, Zorn and the other musicians and colleagues, who have always accompanied him on his musical journey, have developed a sort of schizophrenia that allows them to draw energy and inspiration from New York in the form of an irrational fantasy and, at the same time, merge their unpublished theorems into a series of strictly logical passages. The secret of Zorn's success is an absolute domination of the pragmatic fantasy language that gives his music the ambition of being able to overcome the problem of congestion with the appearance of objectivity. Zorn manages to reconcile the needs of fantasies and concreteness of his interpreters with the dreams of a culture of congestion of our post-modernist and contemporary era. With Zorn, efficacy is intertwined with the sublime. Zorn aims to the paradox of maximum congestion combined with maximum beauty.

The end

Memories are sellective. The most important things can be forgotten because our unconscious is in contrast with them. We are emotional with our memory. In our life, we filter, select things. Historical memory is also changed, like social and collective memory, influenced by the media. In the past there was a continuity between life in the family, at school and at work, in the village or in the city, helping to create a common collective memory of the moment and the past. Today we tend to get rid of things quickly, as well as our memories.

Our culture in recent decades has shown a worrying trend towards the accumulation of cultural gestures, making this accumulation dripping with meanings and cumbersome to the point of urgently posing the problem of its use as a potentially restructuring material. The Book Of Heads represents a reference to a primary level of articulation of given cultural elements. Berio states that "After Webern, the impact and complexity of our sound continuum seem to discourage any systematic attempt to order it in a generalized linguistic perspective; the scholastic opposition between "nature / culture" definitively loses its importance: each work presents itself as a phonological system given with its specific set of distinctive features that must be studied and understood in their specific functions within a given poetics"[124].

A stubborn tradition paints the aesthetic attitude as a passive contemplation of the immediate data, direct apprehension of what is presented, uncontaminated by any conceptualization, isolated from all the echoes of the past and from all the threats and promises of the future, free from any initiative. But the aesthetic experience is dynamic and not static. It is necessary to make delicate discriminations and see subtle relationships, identify symbolic systems and characteristics proper to these systems and what these characters exemplify, interpret works and reorganize the world in terms of music and music in terms of the world.

---

[124] Luciano Berio, Scritti sulla musica, pag. 59 (translation is mine).

The aesthetic attitude is a mobile attitude, research, exploration, it is less attitude than action: creation and re-creation.

Why should I publish a book on The Book Of Heads more than 20 years after their first recording and almost 40 years after their creation in an era that continues to disdain manifestos? It may seem out of date, but I believe that the role of being outdated is the one best suited to those involved in contemporary culture: it's a continuous matter of balance and coordination and also something almost spiritual. This is the essence of music: it's the social act par excellence. Every interpretation, every decision, every step we take is carried out in relation to an idea. We are not referring to an open set of codes. One of the best known and perhaps superficial aspects of these codes is musical notation, which has confused many people when scores appeared that no longer featured five-line staves, traditional notes, etc. We asked ourselves hastily if it wasn't a chance, a simple throw of dice in the air. It's certainly not about this, but about the process that is needed to obtain a certain musical result in relation to an idea. It's not a question of freedom, but of rigor. The Book Of Heads is a work where there is a sense of accumulation and convergence of different energies (musical, dramaturgical, moral, cultural and social). Form and content. Form and substance. Form and function.

In The Book Of Heads what is considered as avantgarde has reached levels of refinement, complexity and theatricality rarely achieved before.

Zorn with BOH has created:

a theory that works;
a mania that catches;
a wish that has become reality;
an open work that its interpreters can continue and change.

Acknowledgments

This book has reached its present form with time, with the accumulation of materials, readings and thanks to many people and various circumstances. My unlimited thanks go first of all to John Zorn, without whose creativity and inventiveness this book would obviously not have been written. My most sincere thanks and best wishes to him to continue like this, to continue composing, producing, playing, recording and still spreading so much beautiful music.
Many thanks to Alessandra Novaga. Thank you for your friendship, for your nice foreward and for being the first to play in Italy the full edition of The Book Of Heads. So many ideas about this book were born from our chats and from the emails we exchanged.
Thanks to all those who performed The Book Of Heads, a composition remains frozen in the paper without its interpreters, without those who animate it every time giving it new life.
So thanks to Doctor Eugene Chadbourne, without whom these studies would not have been born, thanks for your wonderful anarchy.
Thanks to Marc Ribot, for having reinterpreted and recorded them in 1995, bringing back the interest on them and for having performed them on the evening of December 3, 1999 in Venice. Thanks again for triggering this beautiful obsession.
Thanks to Marco Cappelli for having interpreted some studies in his "Yun Mu" and for having believed in it so much that he wanted to move to New York. Thanks for your laughs and your friendship. I'll wait for you in Venice for another wine tour.
Thanks to Christoph Funabashi, for your great cd. Your new interpretation has opened me up to new ideas and possibilities.
Thanks to James Moore for your new full edition twenty years after Marc Ribot's. Thanks for your musical theater and for your vision.
Thanks to all of you who have ventured with these studies and who have crowded my evenings on Youtube: Sergio Sorrentino, Elena Càsoli,

Ericsson Castro, Chris Moy, John Birt, Kobe Van Cauwenberghe, Alex Nauman, Matt Smiley, to name but a few.

Thanks to my family: thanks to Serena and Nicola, I can't say enough. You have lived with me and with this project all the time, thanks for reminding me when it was time to turn off the computer and stop reading and reasoning about it. This book is dedicated to you.

Discography

JOHN ZORN

John Zorn, The Big Gundown, Nonesuch, 1986
John Zorn, Cobra, Hat Hut Records, 1987
John Zorn, Spillane, Elektra Nonesuch, 1987
John Zorn, Spy Vs. Spy: The Music Of Ornette Coleman, Nonesuch, 1988
John Zorn/George Lewis/Bill Frisell, News For Lulu, hat ART, 1988
John Zorn, Naked City, Elektra Nonesuch, 1990
Naked City, Torture Garden, Shimmy Disc, 1990
Carl Stalling, The Carl Stalling Project (Music From Warner Bros. Cartoons 1936-1958), Warner Bros. Records, 1990
John Zorn, Cobra (Live), hat ART, 1991
Carl Stalling, The Carl Stalling Project Volume 2 (More Music From Warner Bros. Cartoons 1939-1957), Warner Bros. Records, 1995
John Zorn, Elegy, Tzadik, 1995
John Zorn, Kristallnacht, Tzadik, 1995
John Zorn, Cobra Tokyo Operations '94, Avant, 1995
John Zorn, John Zorn's Cobra: Live At The Knitting Factory, Knitting Factory Works, 1995
John Zorn, The Bribe - Variations And Extensions On Spillane, Tzadik, 1998
John Zorn, Locus Solus, Tzadik, 1997
John Zorn, The Parachute Years 1977 - 1980 (Lacrosse Hockey Pool Archery), Tzadik, 1997
John Zorn, Godard / Spillane, Tzadik, 1999
John Zorn, Cobra, Tzadik, 2002
Claudia Heuermann, A Bookshelf on Top of the Sky: 12 Stories About John Zorn, Tzadik, 2004
John Zorn, Filmworks Anthology - 20 Years Of Soundtrack Music,

Tzadik, 2005
Naked City, Complete Studio Recordings, Tzadik 2005
Ken Jacobs/John Zorn, Celestial Subway Lines/Salvaging Noise (DVD, NTSC), Tzadik, 2005
John Zorn/ Richard Foreman/Henry Hills, Astronome: A Night At The Opera (A Disturbing Initiation) - Ontological-Hysteric Theater, Vol. 2 (DVD, NTSC, Col), Tzadik 2010

THE BOOK OF HEADS

Eugene Chadbourne; Volume One: Solo Acoustic Guitar, Parachute, 1976
Eugene Chadbourne; Volume Two: Solo Acoustic Guitar, Parachute, 1976
Eugene Chadbourne; Volume Three: Guitar Trios, Parachute, 1977
John Zorn, The Book Of Heads feautirng Marc Ribot, Tzadik, 1995
Eugene Chadbourne, John Zorn, 1977 1981, Materiali Sonori, 1998
Marco Cappelli, Yun Mu, Teatro Del Sole, 2002
Christoph Funabashi, John Zorn: The Book Of Heads, Schraum, 2012
James Moore, James Moore Plays The Book Of Heads (CD And DVD Of A Film By Stephen Taylor), Tzadik, 2015

Bibliography

Aguzzi Andrea, Chitarre Visionarie Conversazioni con chitarristi alternativi, Youcanprint, 2014
Aguzzi Andrea, Visionary Guitars Chatting with Guitarists, Lulu.com, 2016.
Associazione Cinematografica Pandora (a cura di Borroni Marco, Brianzoli Giorgia), John Zorn Filmworks, GS Editrice, Milano, 2000.
Attali Jacques, Noise: The Political Economy of Music, Calder & Boyars, University Press, Manchester, 1985.
Bailey Derek, Improvisation: Its Nature and Practise In Music, The British Library, London, 1992
Barthes Roland, Image Music Text, Fontana Press, Glasgow, 1990
Barthes Roland, L'impero dei segni, Einaudi, Torino, 2002
Barthes Roland, L'ovvio e l'ottuso, Einaudi, Torino, 2002
Bennett Andy, Dawe Kevin, Guitar Cultures, Berg, Oxford, 2001.
Bruno Giuliana, Atlante delle emozioni: in viaggio tra arte, architettura e cinema, Pearson Italia S.p.a., 2006.
Bruno Giuliana, Superfici. A proposito di estetica, materialità e media, Johan & Levi, 2016.
Cage John, Silence, Wesleyan University Press, Middletown, 1973.
Cauduro Andrea, John Zorn: The Book Of Heads, thesis at Conservatorio di Musica Alfredo Casella, 2019.
Chick Stevie, Psychic Confusion. La storia dei Sonic Youth, Arcana, Roma, 2009
Cox Christoph, Warner Daniel, Audio Culture: Readings in Modern Music, The Continuum International Publishing Group ltd, London, 2006.
Danto Arthur Coleman, Dopo la fine dell'arte. L'arte contemporanea e il confine della storia, Mondadori Bruno, 2008.
Deleuze Gilles e Guattari Felix, Mille piani. Capitalismo e schizofrenia, Castelvecchi, Roma, 2003.

Dorlfles Gino, Ultime tendenze nell'arte d'oggi: dall'informale al neo-oggettuale, Feltrinelli Editore, Milano, 1999
Dorlfles Gino, Itinerario estetico: simbolo, mito, metafora, Editrice Compositori, Bologna, 2011
Dorlfles Gino, Horror pleni: la (in)civiltà del rumore, Alberto Castelvecchi Editore srl, Roma, 2008.
Duckworth William, Talking Music: Conversations With John Cage, Philip Glass, Laurie Anderson, And 5 Generations Of American Experimental Composers, Da Capo Press, Boston, 1999.
Eco Umberto, Opera aperta. Forma e indeterminazione nelle poetiche contemporanee, Bompiani, Milano, 2000
Eco Umberto, Il Nome Della Rosa, Bompiani, Milano, 1984
Eco Umberto, Dire quasi la stessa cosa: Esperienze di traduzione, Bompiani, Milano, 2013
Eco Umberto, I limiti dell'interpretazione, La Nave di Teseo Editore SPA, Milano, 2016.
Ghezzi Enrico, Sgarbi Elisabetta (a cura di), Panta Musica, Bompiani, Milano, 1999.
Gloag Kenneth, Postmodernism in Music, Cambridge Univeristy Press, Cambridge, 2012.
Goodman Nelson, I linguaggi dell'arte, Il Saggiatore, Milano, 2008
Gordon Kim, Is it My Body?: Selected Texts, Sternberg Press, 2014
Gordon Kim, Girl in a Band. L'autobiografia, Minimum Fax, 2016.
Gottschalk Jennie, Experimental Music Since 1970, Bloomsbury Publishing USA, New York, 2016.
Gould Glenn, The Glenn Gould Reader, Knopf, New York, 1984.
Harper Adam, Infinite Music: Imaging The Next Millennium of Human Music-Making, Zero Book, Winchester, 2011.
Hegarty Paul, Noise Music: A History, The Continuum International Publishing Group ltd, London, 2007.
Heller Michael C., Loft Jazz: Improvising New York in the 1970s, University of California Press, Oakland, 2017
Hermes Will, New York 1973-1977. Cinque anni che hanno rivoluzionato

la musica, Codice, 2014.
Homberg Eric, New York City, Bruno Mondadori, Milano, 2003.
Johnson Tom, The Voice of the New Music New York City 1972 – 1982, 1989
Jones Andrew, Plunderphonics, 'Pataphysic & Pop Mechanics an introduction to musique actuelle, Redwood Books, Trowbridge, 1995
Koolhaas Rem, Delirious New York: un manifesto retroattivo per Manhattan, Electa, Milano, 2002.
Kramer Jonathan D., Beyond Unity: Toward an Understanding of Musical Postmodernism, in Concert music, rock, and jazz since 1945: essays and analytical studies, London and New York, Routledge, 2002
Lowell Brackett John, John Zorn: Tradition and Transgression, Indiana University Press, 2008.
Maffi Mario, La cultura underground I. Dai beats agli yippies, Laterza, 1980
Maffi Mario, La cultura underground I. Dai beats agli yippies, Laterza, Roma, 1980.
Maffi Mario, La cultura underground II. Rock, poesia, cinema, teatro, Laterza, Roma, 1980.
Maffi Mario, New York Ritratto di una città, Odoya srl, Bologna, 2004.
McCutchan Ann, The Muse that Sings: Composers Speak about the Creative Process, Oxford University Press, 2003.
Merlin Enrico, 1000 Dischi per un Secolo: 1900-2000, Il Saggiatore, Milano, 2012.
Miles Barry, I Settanta, Il Saggiatore, Milano, 2014.
Molinari Maurizio, Gli Ebrei di New York, Laterza, Roma, 2007.
Nyman Michael, Experimental Music: Cage and Beyond, Cambridge University Press, Cambridge,1999.
Paci Dalò Roberto, Quinz Emanuele, Millesuoni: Deleuze, Guattari e la musica elettronica, Cronopio, Napoli, 2006.
Pivato Stefano, Il secolo del rumore: il paesaggio sonoro nel Novecento, Il Mulino, Bologna, 2011.
Principato Maurizio, John Zorn: musicista, compositore, esploratore,

Casanova e Chianura edizioni, Milano, 2011.
Ross Alex, Il resto è rumore. Ascoltando il XX secolo, Bompiani, Milano, 2009.
Ross Alex, Senti questo, Bompiani, Milano, 2011.
Rovere Walter, Chiti Carla, John Zorn, Sonora Itinerari Oltre Il Suono, Materiali Sonori Edizioni Musicali, S.Giovanni Valdarno, 1998
Rutherford-Johnson Tim, Music after the Fall: Modern Composition and Culture since 1989, University of California Press, Oakland, 2017.
Shapiro Peter, You should be dancing. Biografia politica della discomusic, Kowalski, 2007
Sontag Susan, Against Interpretation and Other Essays, Penguin UK, 2013
Sontag Susan, Interpretazioni tendenziose: dodici temi culturali, Einaudi, Torino, 1975
Sontag Susan, Odio sentirmi una vittima. Intervista su amore, dolore e scrittura con Jonathan Cott, Il Saggiatore, Milano, 2016
Sontag Susan, Sulla fotografia: realtà e immagine nella nostra società, Einaudi, Torino, 2004.
Sorrentino Sergio, La Chitarra Elettrica nella Musica da Concerto, Arcana, Roma, 2019.
Sparti Davide, Suoni inauditi: l'improvvisazione nel jazz e nella vita quotidiana, Il Mulino, Bologna, 2005
Stubbs David, Fear of Music: Why People Get Rothko But Don't Get Stockhausen, Zero Book, Winchester, 2009.
Toop David, Ocean of Sound: Aether Talk, Ambient Sound and Imaginary Worlds, Serpent's Tail, London, 1995.
Toop David, Haunted Weather: Music, Silence, and Memory, Serpent's Tail, London, 2004.
Toop David, Into the Maelstrom: Music, Improvisation and the Dream of Freedom: Before 1970, Bloomsbury Publishing USA, 2016.
Young Rob, La guida alla musica moderna di Wire, Isbn Edizioni, 2010.
Zorn John, Arcana: Musicians on Music, Hips Road, New York, 2000.
Zorn John, Arcana II: Musicians on Music, Hips Road, New York, 2007.

Zorn John, Arcana III: Musicians on Music, Hips Road, New York, 2008.
Zorn John, Arcana IV: Musicians on Music, Hips Road, New York, 2009.
Zorn John, Arcana V: Musicians on Music, Hips Road, New York, 2010.
Zorn John, Arcana VI: Musicians on Music, Hips Road, New York, 2012.
Zorn John, Arcana VII: Musicians on Music, Hips Road, New York, 2014.
Zorn John, Arcana VIII: Musicians on Music, Hips Road, New York, 2017.